THE COMPLETE BOOK

Chords
Scales
Arpeggios
For The Guitarist

by Al Politano

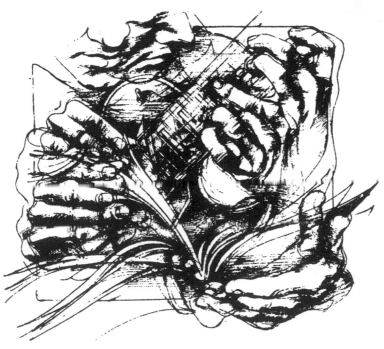

Calligraphy by George Ports
Cover Art and Layout by Mark Ulves
Production by Ron Middlebrook

ISBN 978-0-89898-217-6

Centerstream Publishing - P. O. Box 17878 - Anaheim Hills, CA 92807 U. S. A.
Phone/fax (714) 779-9390

About the Author

Al Politano was born in Pittsburgh, Pennsylvania and has studied guitar since the age of six. He has performed in most every kind of musical situation, from studio work and union jazz bands to classical recitals. His academic achievements include a B.A. degree in musical education from Californaia State University, as well as a teaching credential in music. He has taught guitar since 1964 and recently has gained public recognition through his guitar publications and his clinics and workshops at prominent colleges and universities. He has spent a lifetime not only dedicated to the guitar, but dedicated to the ideas of improving the teaching and facilitating the learning of the instrument.

PREFACE

After years of teaching the guitar, I noticed that there was a need for a complete book of chords, arpeggios and scales. Granted, there are other books which deal with the same subject matter. but they generally give only one position of the chords, arpeggios and scales. In this book, they are plotted out in every practical position, and with some dedicated study, one could play all the chords, arpeggios and scales in *every position* and in *every key* with the aid of this book.

This book may be used as a reference book, or it is hoped that the guitar teacher will assign a few chords, arpeggios or scales each week to a student.

This book is written with a minimum amount of verbalization. I wanted to present the reader, who I assume is a musician or a person with a musical sense, with just "the facts" and leave it to the reader to use the material for the betterment of his or her own playing. Whether this book is used for improvising, study or exercises is totally up to the teacher/musician using it, and it is hoped that you, as a guitarist, will gain greatly from this book.

Al Politano

Table of Contents

HOW TO READ THE GRIDS

The grids represent the frets on the fingerboard of the guitar and are written in one of two ways:

For Chords
For Arpeggios and Scales

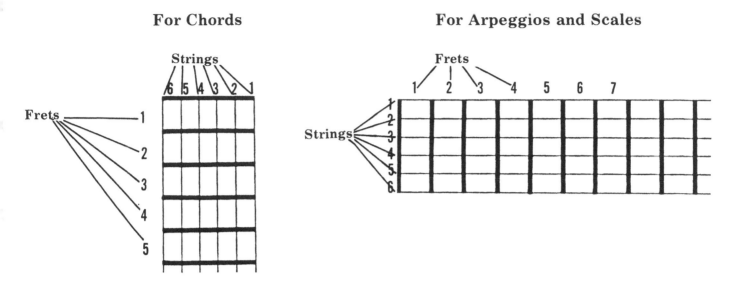

Numbers inside the grids represent the fingers to be used. "Zeros" (0) above the chord grid indicate that the string is to be played open. If nothing appears above a particular string or an "X" is written, *do not play that string.*

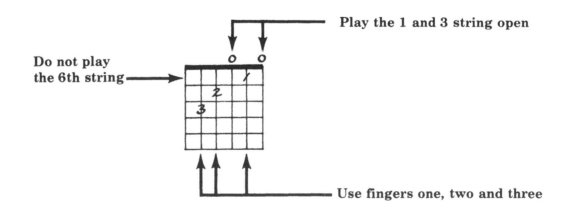

Play the 1 and 3 string open

Do not play
the 6th string

Use fingers one, two and three

Numbers underneath a particular grid indicate an alternate fingering.

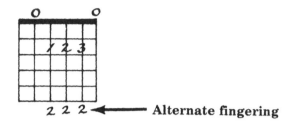

Alternate fingering

Barring is indicated by a straight line or a repeated finger number.

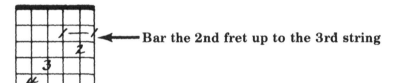

◄—Bar the 2nd fret up to the 3rd string

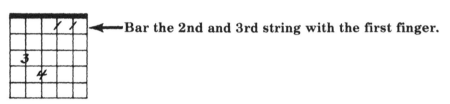

◄—Bar the 2nd and 3rd string with the first finger.

Notes that extend beyond the fifth fret are indicated in this way.

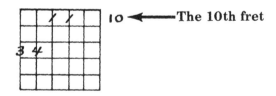

10 ◄—The 10th fret

The number beside the grid indicates the starting fret

Transposing The Forms

Except for the section on "Open Position Chords", every other chord, arpeggio and scale is moveable to all keys.

To transpose the forms, first find the "R" which will indicate the root of the chord. After finding the "R" on a particular string, **the note closest to the "R" will be the root.**

Root is on the 6th string, 1st fret "F". ——→
The name of this chord is "F"

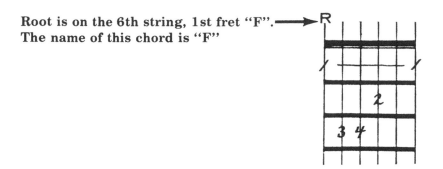

Root is on the 5th string 2nd fret "B". ————————→ R
The name of this scale is "B"

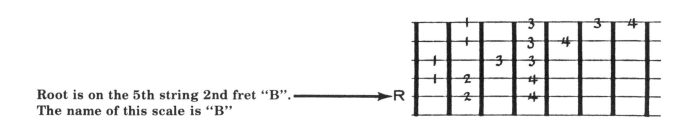

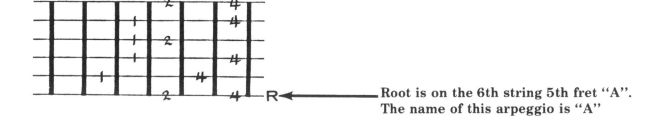

R ←———————— **Root is on the 6th string 5th fret "A".**
The name of this arpeggio is "A"

By moving the exact fingering of the grid up or down the neck, each position change will assume a different name.

Move up the chord one fret and the chord becomes "F#", if moved up again it becomes "G", and so on. . .

GUITAR FINGERBOARD
CHART

If your not familiar with the names of the notes on the fingerboard, the chart below will aid in naming the root. The corresponding note on the musical staff is also given.

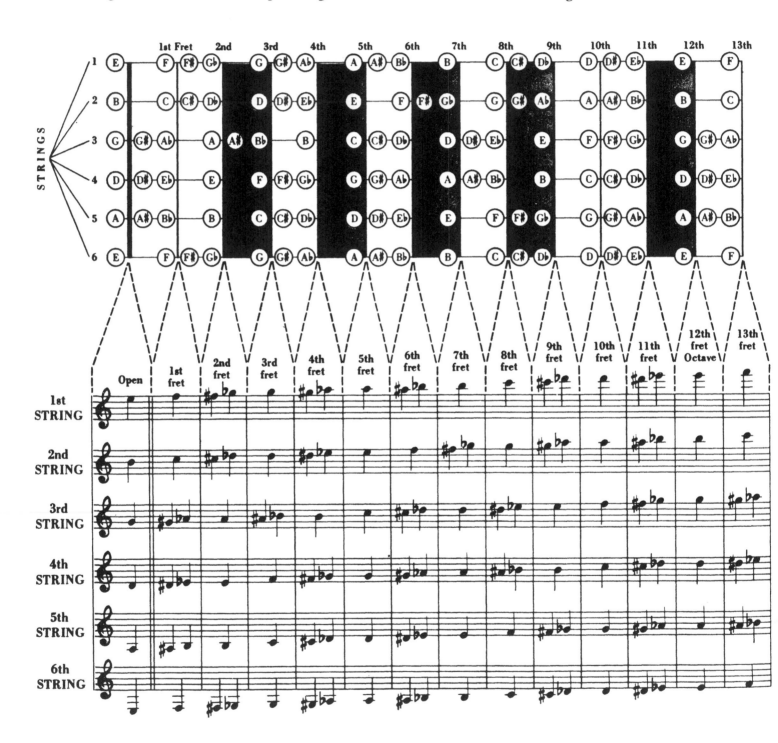

CHORD THEORY

A chord is composed of three or more notes. A chord can either be played together (harmonically) or each note can be played separately which is called an arpeggio. Although any interval can be imposed on top of each other to form a chord, most chords are built in thirds. This system of building chords in thirds is called tertian harmony.

To identify the make-up of a chord it is customary to apply numbers to the notes in the chord. These numbers are taken from the chord's corresponding major scale starting from the root (first tone) and going to the thirteenth tone.

Each chord will have a different formula, if a tone is to be LOWERED a Flat sign (♭), or a minus sign (−) is used. If the tone is to be RAISED a Sharp sign (♯), or a Plus sign (+) is used. The following chart will outline the chord formulas and give their common symbols. (All examples are in the key of "C").

TRIADS

Traids are three note chords and provide the foundation for all other chords.

Name	Formula	Symbols

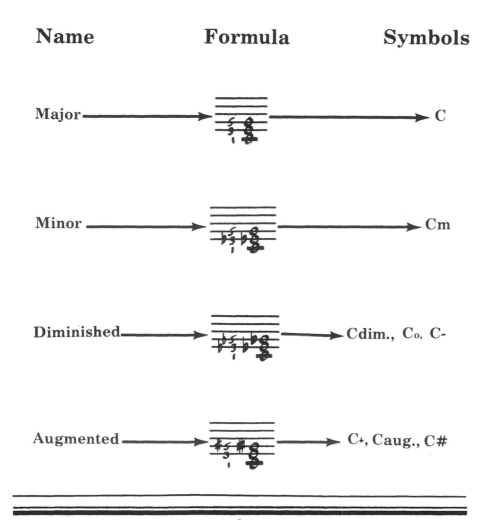

CHORDS OF ADDITION

Chords of Addition are major or minor triads with the addition of a sixth or ninth tone or both. The suspended fourth chord has a different make-up: it's third is omitted and a fourth is added. because of this addition it is included here.

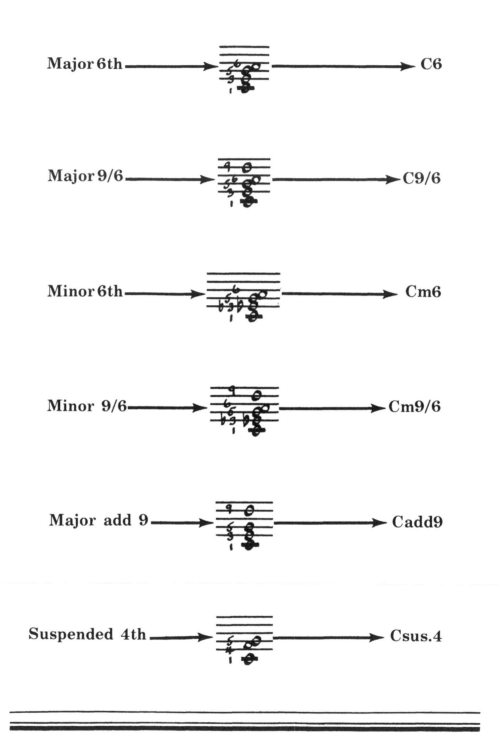

Major 6th → C6

Major 9/6 → C9/6

Minor 6th → Cm6

Minor 9/6 → Cm9/6

Major add 9 → Cadd9

Suspended 4th → Csus.4

SEVENTH CHORDS

Seventh Chords will have another third imposed onto a given triad making a four note chord.

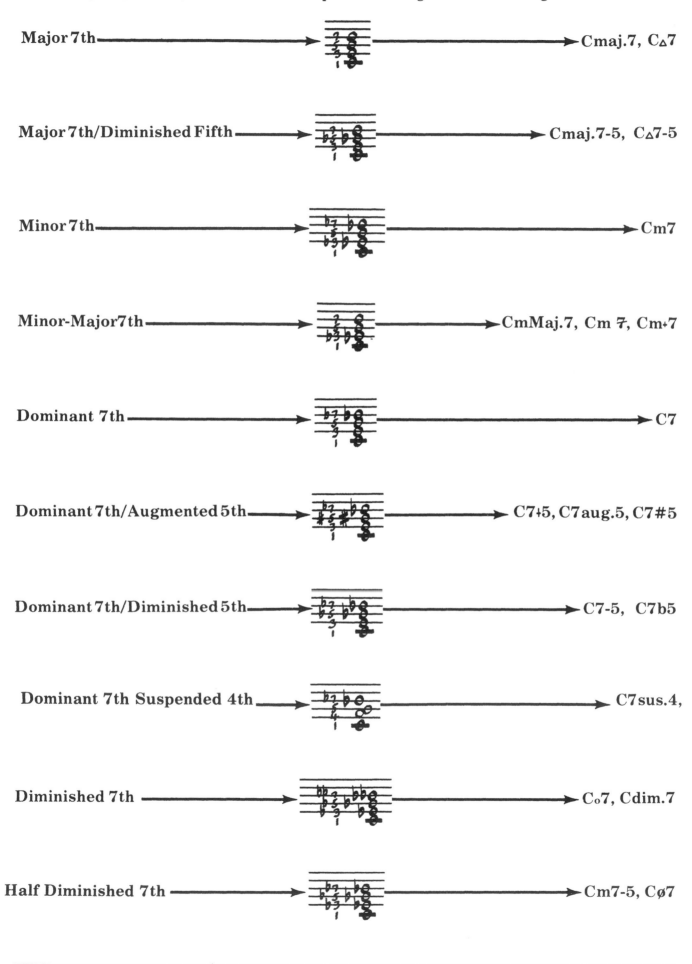

Major 7th — Cmaj.7, C△7

Major 7th/Diminished Fifth — Cmaj.7-5, C△7-5

Minor 7th — Cm7

Minor-Major 7th — CmMaj.7, Cm7, Cm+7

Dominant 7th — C7

Dominant 7th/Augmented 5th — C7+5, C7aug.5, C7#5

Dominant 7th/Diminished 5th — C7-5, C7b5

Dominant 7th Suspended 4th — C7sus.4,

Diminished 7th — C°7, Cdim.7

Half Diminished 7th — Cm7-5, Cø7

NINTH CHORDS

Ninth Chords will have the addition of another third above the seventh, making a five note chord

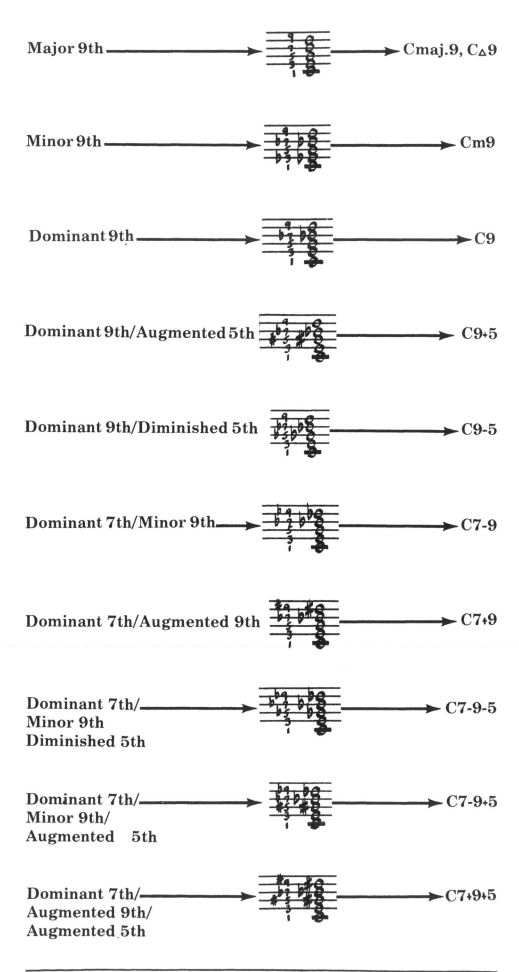

Major 9th	Cmaj.9, C△9
Minor 9th	Cm9
Dominant 9th	C9
Dominant 9th/Augmented 5th	C9+5
Dominant 9th/Diminished 5th	C9-5
Dominant 7th/Minor 9th	C7-9
Dominant 7th/Augmented 9th	C7+9
Dominant 7th/ Minor 9th Diminished 5th	C7-9-5
Dominant 7th/ Minor 9th/ Augmented 5th	C7-9+5
Dominant 7th/ Augmented 9th/ Augmented 5th	C7+9+5

ELEVENTH CHORDS

Eleventh chords are formed by adding a third above the ninth. The eleventh tone will have the same name as a fourth.

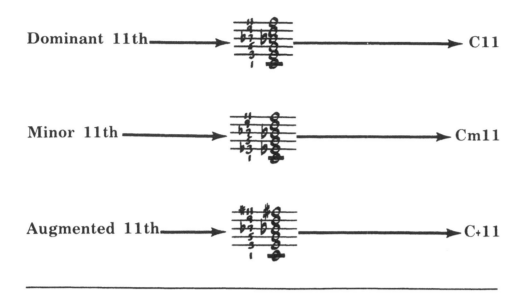

Dominant 11th ⟶ ⟶ C11

Minor 11th ⟶ ⟶ Cm11

Augmented 11th ⟶ ⟶ C+11

THIRTEENTH CHORDS

Thirteenth chords will impose a third above the eleventh. The thirteenth tone will have the same name as a sixth.

Major 13th ⟶ ⟶ Cmaj.13,   C△13

Dominant 13th ⟶ ⟶ C13

Dominant 13th/Minor 9th ⟶ ⟶ C13-9

CHORDS

Chords, primarily chords other than triads, are simplified in certain chord forms since in some cases the theoretical construction is either impractical or undesirable to the ear.

Primarily the fifth and sometimes the root are often omitted from a chord without impairing it's effectiveness. Other tones can be omitted but the essential notes must be left in. For example a ninth chord must contain a ninth.

The third of a chord is omitted in suspended fourth chords and is replaced with the fourth degree of the scale. The third is also often omitted in eleventh chords. The third in most other chords is a very important tone because it designates the tonality of a chord. If the third of a chord is unaltered (a major third) the chord will be of the major type. If the third is lowered the chord will be of the minor type.

In guitar chord forms many tones are doubled or repeated and mixed in a multitude of ways for different voicings.

Chord Inversions

A chord's notes can be mixed so that the notes will be in a different order. This mixing of notes results in different chord inversions.

Chords with the root as the lowest note, are said to be in root position. If the third is the lowest note the chord is in first inversion. If the fifth is the lowest note, the chord is in second inversion.

The example below shows a three note chord (triad) with it's root position and two inversions.

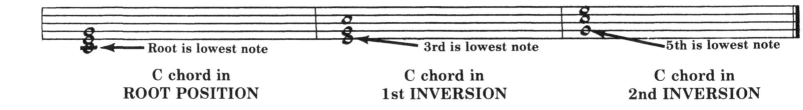

← Root is lowest note	← 3rd is lowest note	← 5th is lowest note
C chord in **ROOT POSITION**	C chord in **1st INVERSION**	C chord in **2nd INVERSION**

All chords have a root position plus a certain amount of inversions depending upon how many notes it has. For example, a Dominant Seventh Chord having four notes has a root position and three inversions. This process can be repeated for ninths, elevenths and thirteenth chords.

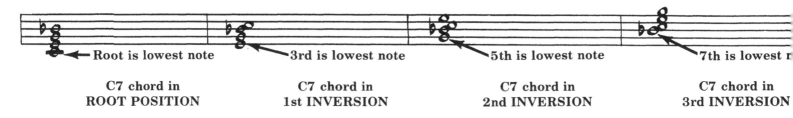

← Root is lowest note	← 3rd is lowest note	← 5th is lowest note	← 7th is lowest r
C7 chord in **ROOT POSITION**	C7 chord in **1st INVERSION**	C7 chord in **2nd INVERSION**	C7 chord in **3rd INVERSION**

The following chords are divided into two groups. First, the OPEN POSITION CHORDS, so-called because each form will contain one or more open strings. The second group will be the MOVEABLE CHORDS and contain no open strings. These chords and their inversions are derived from the sixth, fifth and fourth strings. The root position or inversion can be identified by the "R" or number as indicated on the chord grid.

Open Position Chords
(some forms are not always in root position)

A	Am	Aaug	Asus4	A6	Am6	A7
	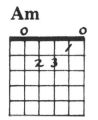	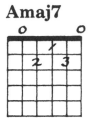	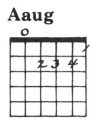	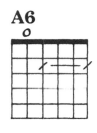	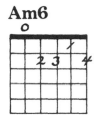	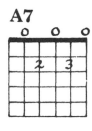

A7sus4	Amaj7	Am7	Adim7	Am7-5	Amaj7-5	Am/maj7
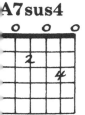	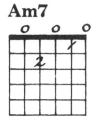	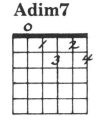	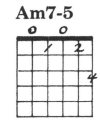	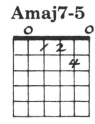	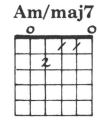	

A7#5	A7-5	A7-9	A7#9	A9	Aadd9	Amaj9
	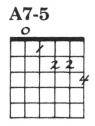	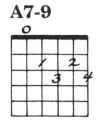	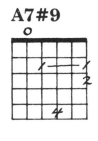	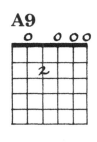	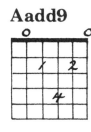	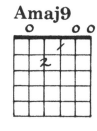

A9/6	Am9	Am9/6	A11	Aaug11	Am11	A13
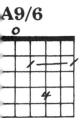	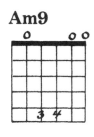	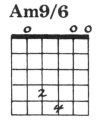	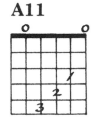	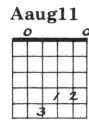	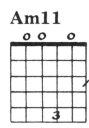	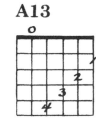

Amaj13	A13-9
	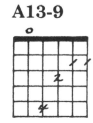

B7	B7sus4	Bdim7	Bm7-5	Bmaj7-5	B7#5	B7-5
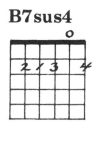	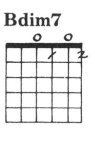	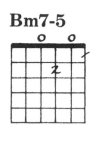	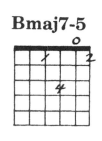	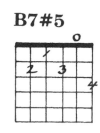	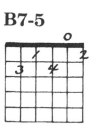	

B11

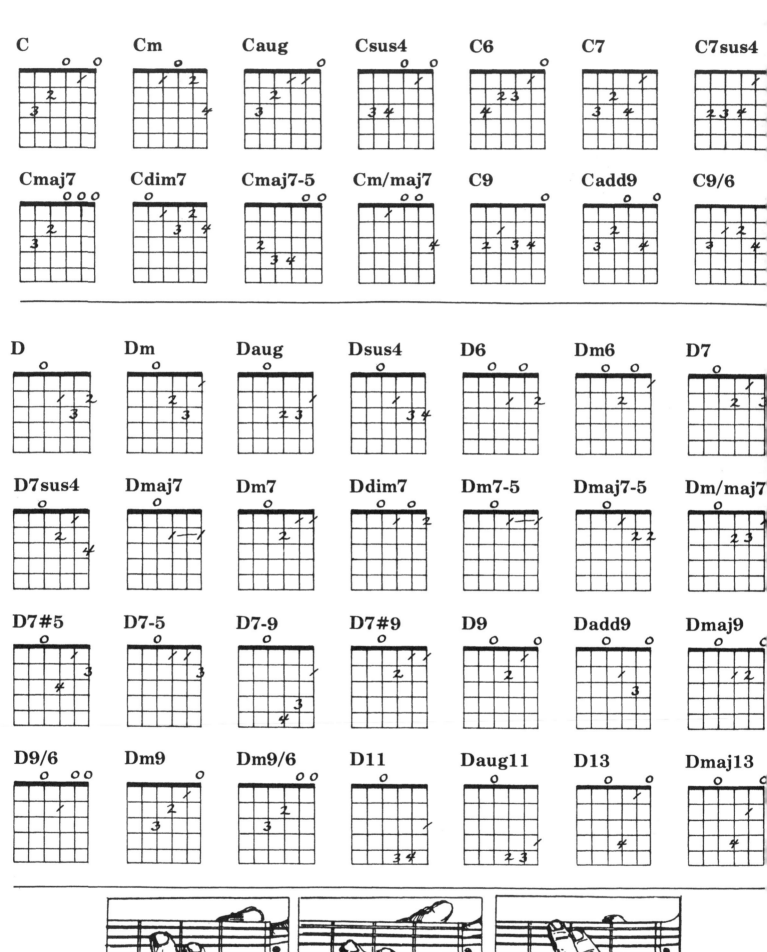

C Cm Caug Csus4 C6 C7 C7sus4

Cmaj7 Cdim7 Cmaj7-5 Cm/maj7 C9 Cadd9 C9/6

D Dm Daug Dsus4 D6 Dm6 D7

D7sus4 Dmaj7 Dm7 Ddim7 Dm7-5 Dmaj7-5 Dm/maj7

D7#5 D7-5 D7-9 D7#9 D9 Dadd9 Dmaj9

D9/6 Dm9 Dm9/6 D11 Daug11 D13 Dmaj13

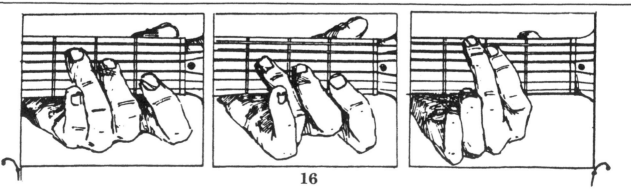

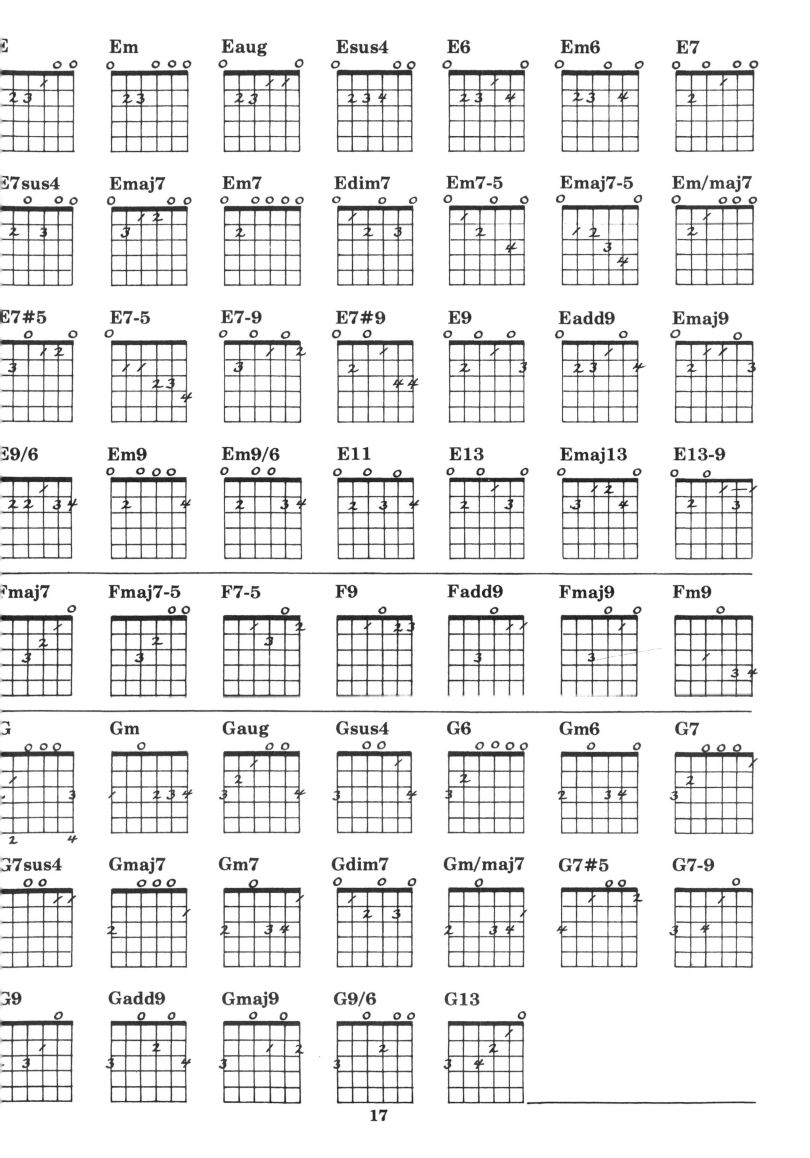

Moveable Chords

Major (1 3 5)

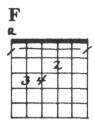
F
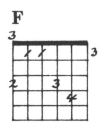
F
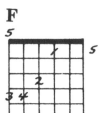
F
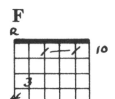
F
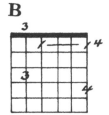
F
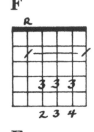
B
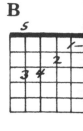
B

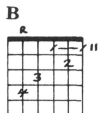
B
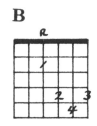
B
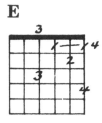
E
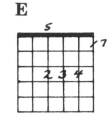
E
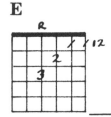
E

Minor (1 -3 5)

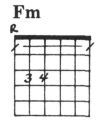
Fm
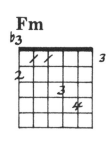
Fm
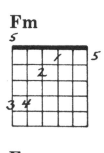
Fm
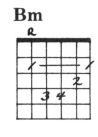
Fm
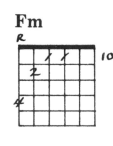
Bm
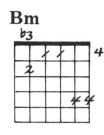
Bm
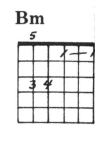
Bm

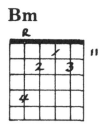
Bm
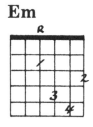
Em
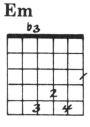
Em
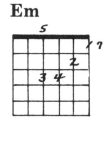
Em
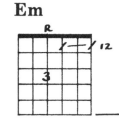
Em

Augmented (1 3 +5)

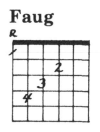
Faug
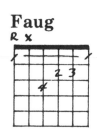
Faug
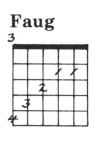
Faug
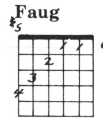
Faug
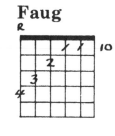
Faug
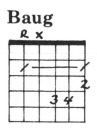
Baug
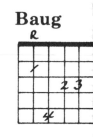
Baug

Baug
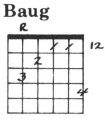
Baug
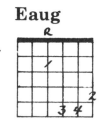
Baug

Eaug
Eaug
Eaug
Eaug

Eaug

18

Suspended 4th (1 4 5)

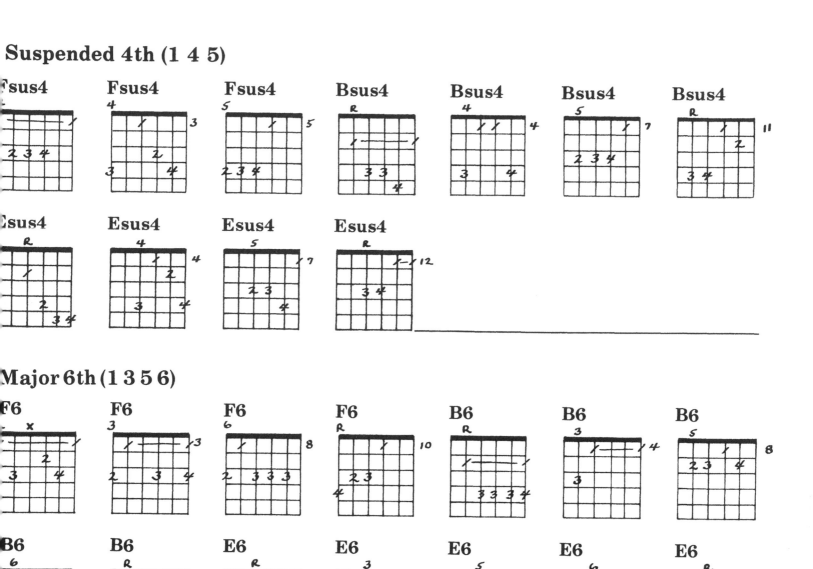

Minor 6th (1 -3 5 6)

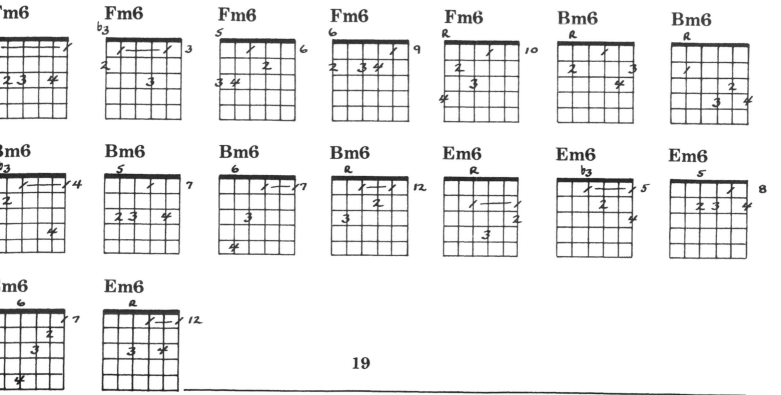

19

Dom. 7th (1 3 5 -7)

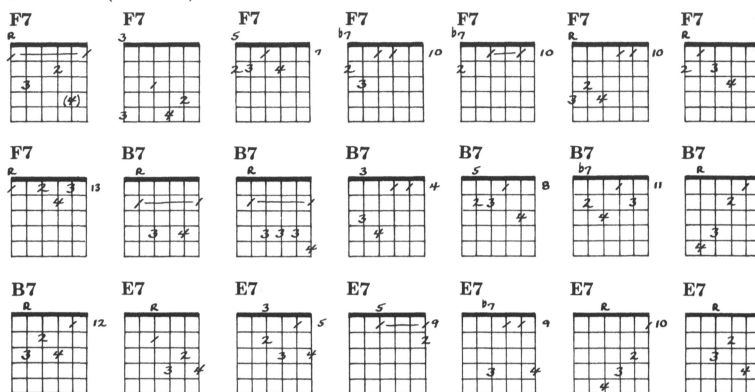

Dom. 7th sus.4 (1 4 5 -7)

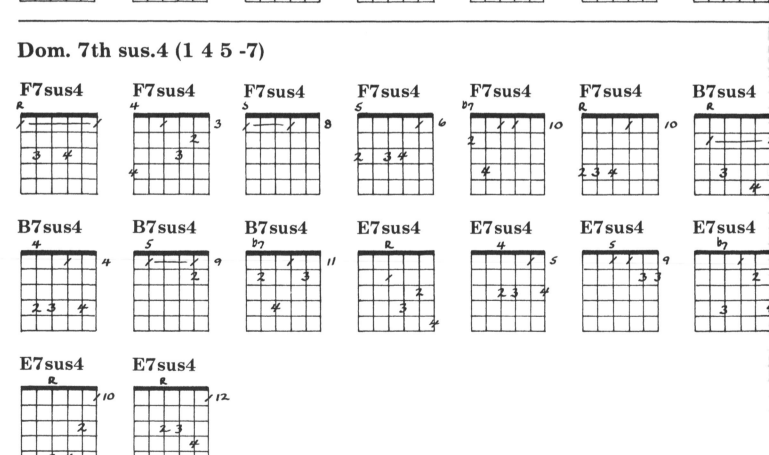

Major 7th (1 3 5 7)

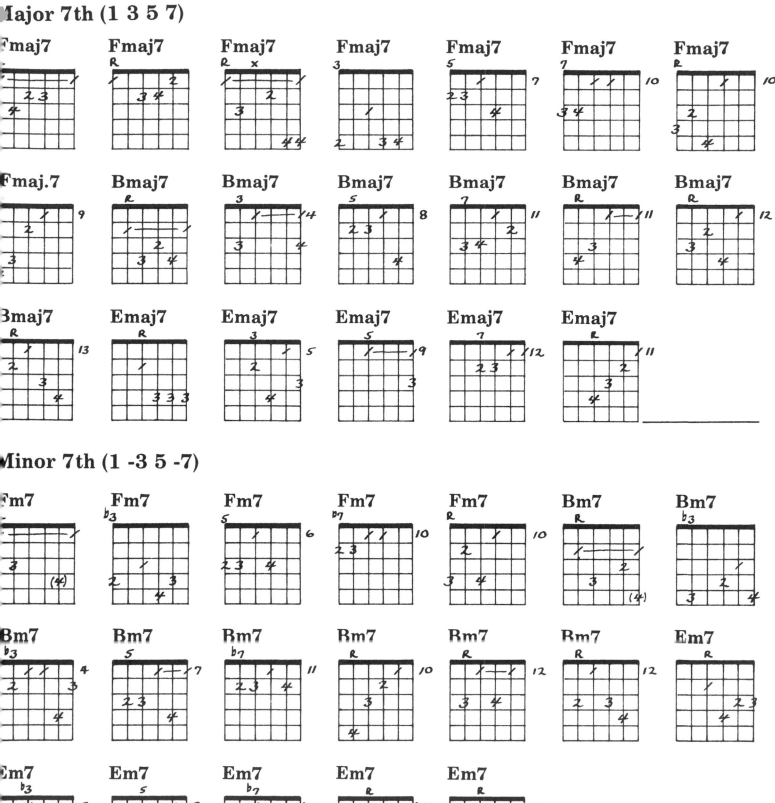

Minor 7th (1 -3 5 -7)

Dim. 7th (1 -3 -5 bb7)

Minor 7-5 (1 -3 -5-7)

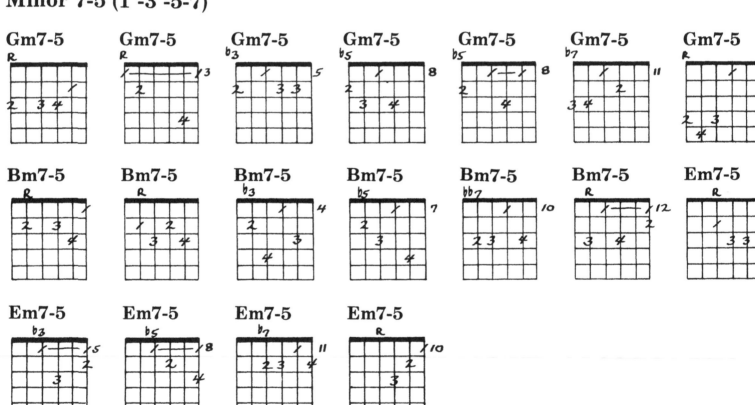

Major 7-5 (1 3 -5 7)

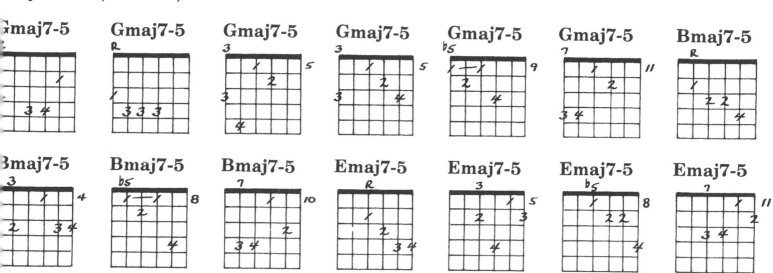

Gmaj7-5   Gmaj7-5   Gmaj7-5   Gmaj7-5   Gmaj7-5   Gmaj7-5   Bmaj7-5

Bmaj7-5   Bmaj7-5   Bmaj7-5   Emaj7-5   Emaj7-5   Emaj7-5   Emaj7-5

Emaj7-5

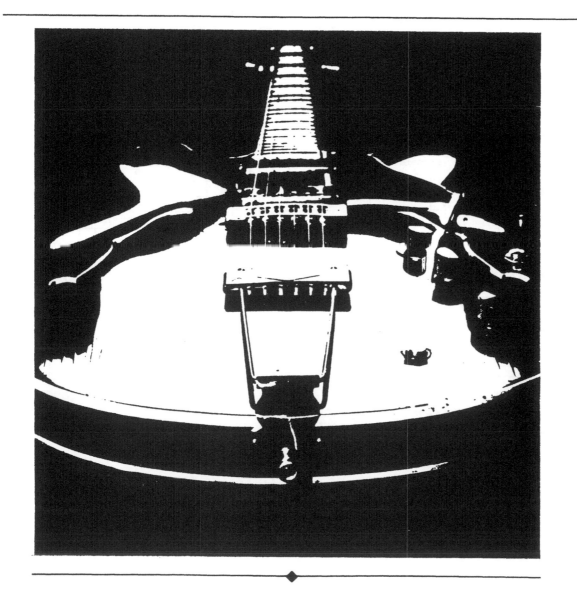

Minor/Major 7th (1 -3 5 7)

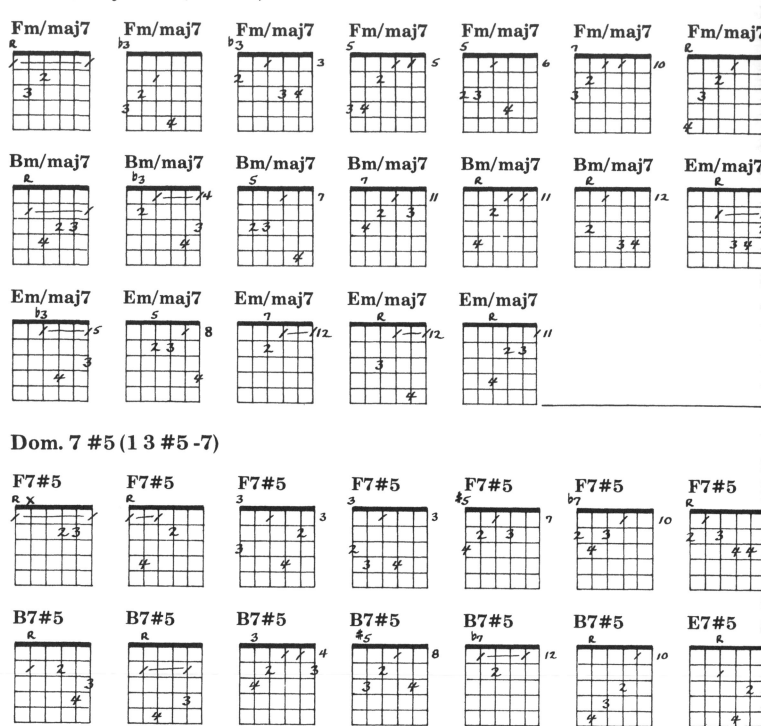

Dom. 7 #5 (1 3 #5 -7)

Dom. 7-5 (1 3 -5 -7)

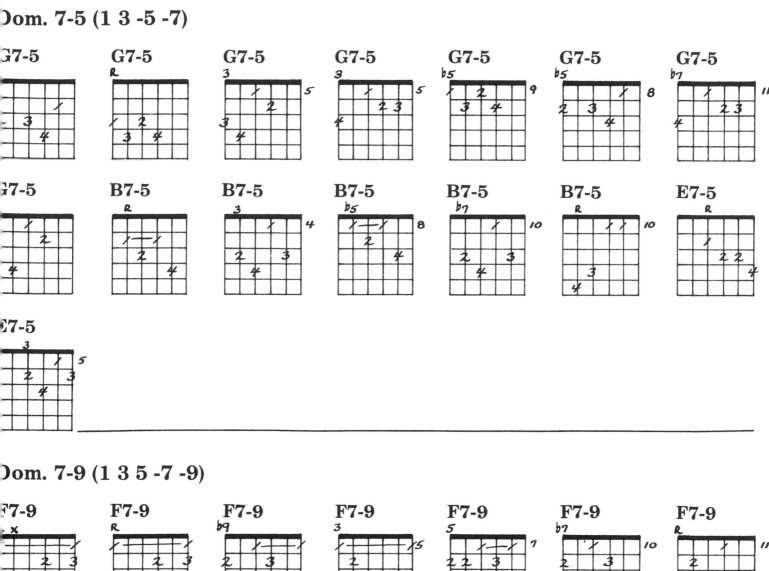

Dom. 7-9 (1 3 5 -7 -9)

Dom. 7#9 (1 3 5 -7 #9)

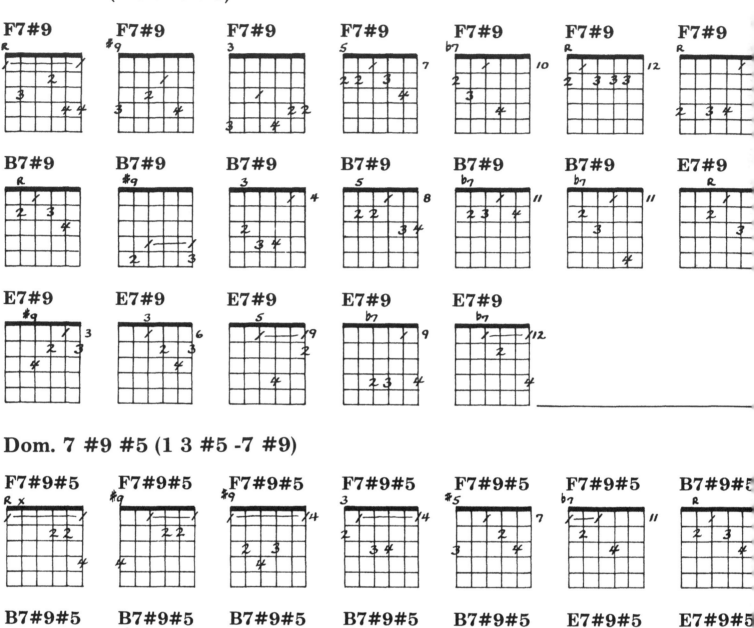

Dom. 7 #9 #5 (1 3 #5 -7 #9)

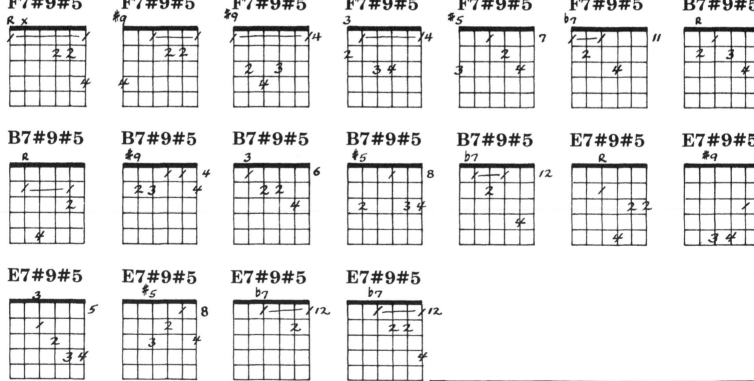

Dom. 7-9#5 (1 3 #5 -7 -9)

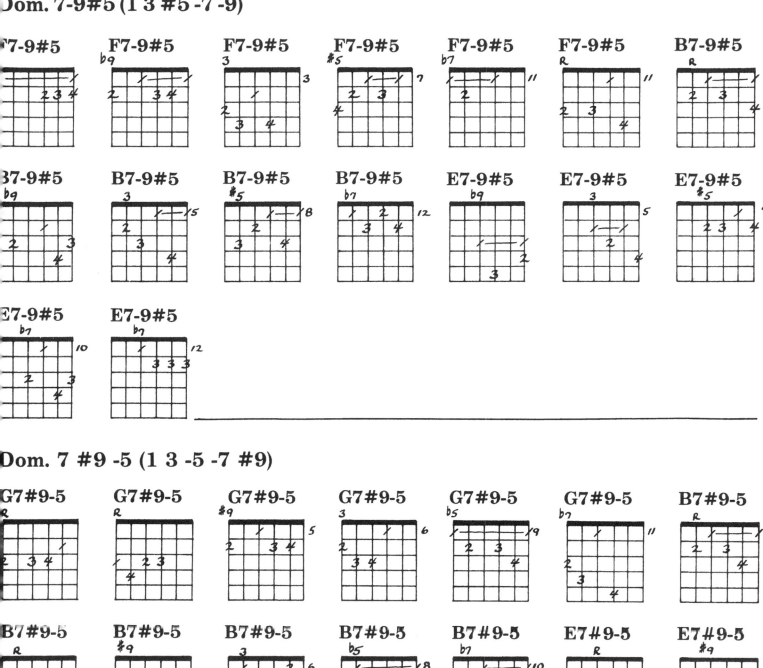

Dom. 7 #9 -5 (1 3 -5 -7 #9)

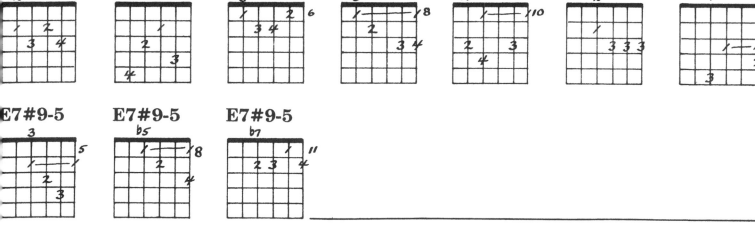

Dom. 7 -9 -5 (1 3 -5 -7 -9)

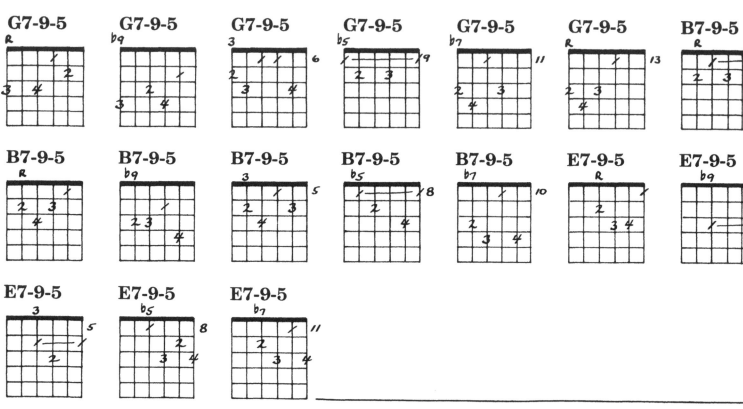

Dom. 9th (1 3 5 -7 9)

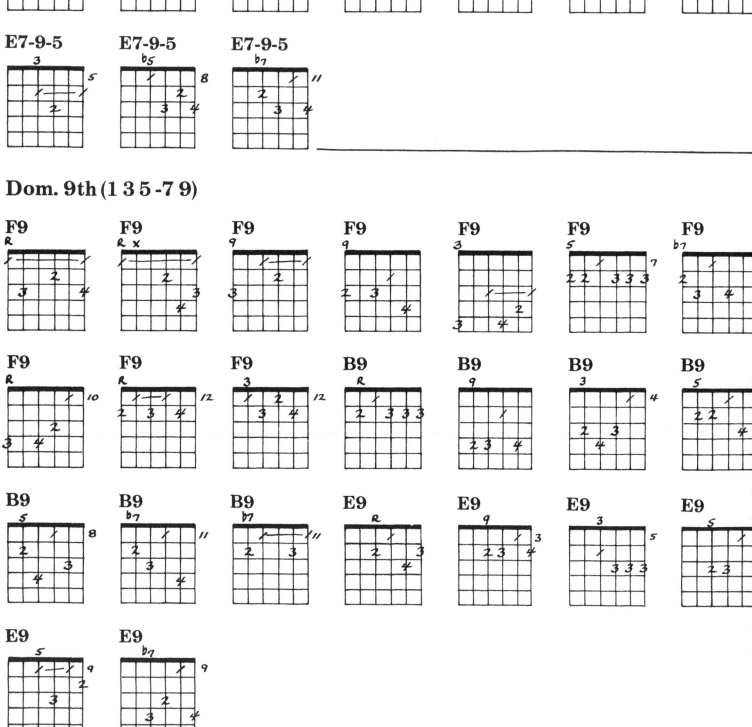

Dom. 9 -5 (1 3 -5 -7 9)

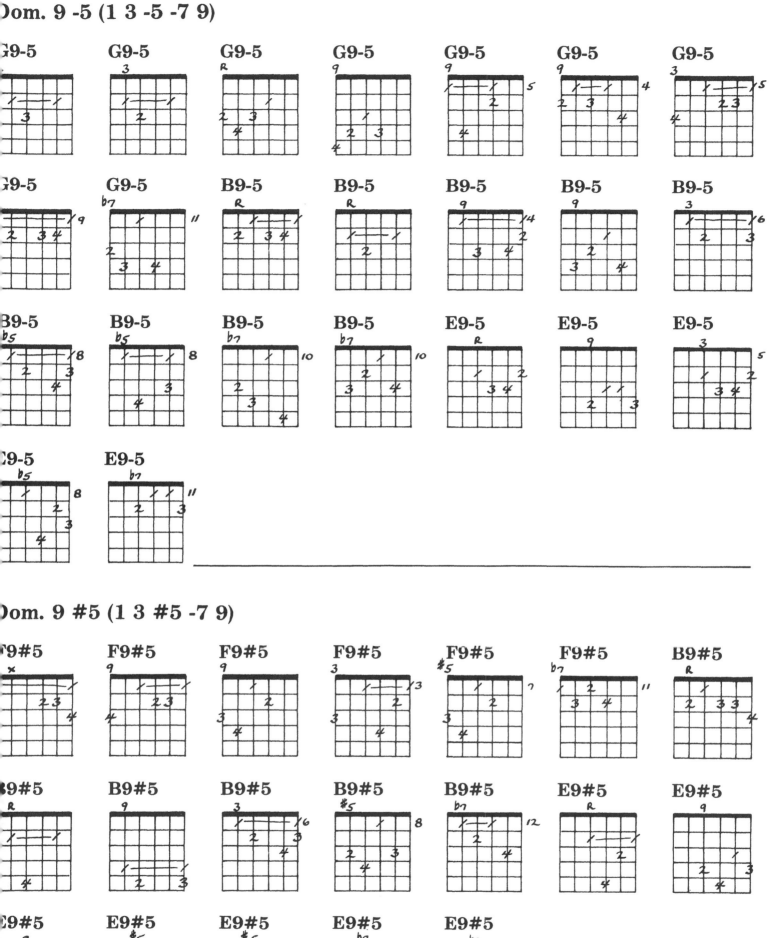

Dom. 9 #5 (1 3 #5 -7 9)

Add 9 (1 3 5 9)

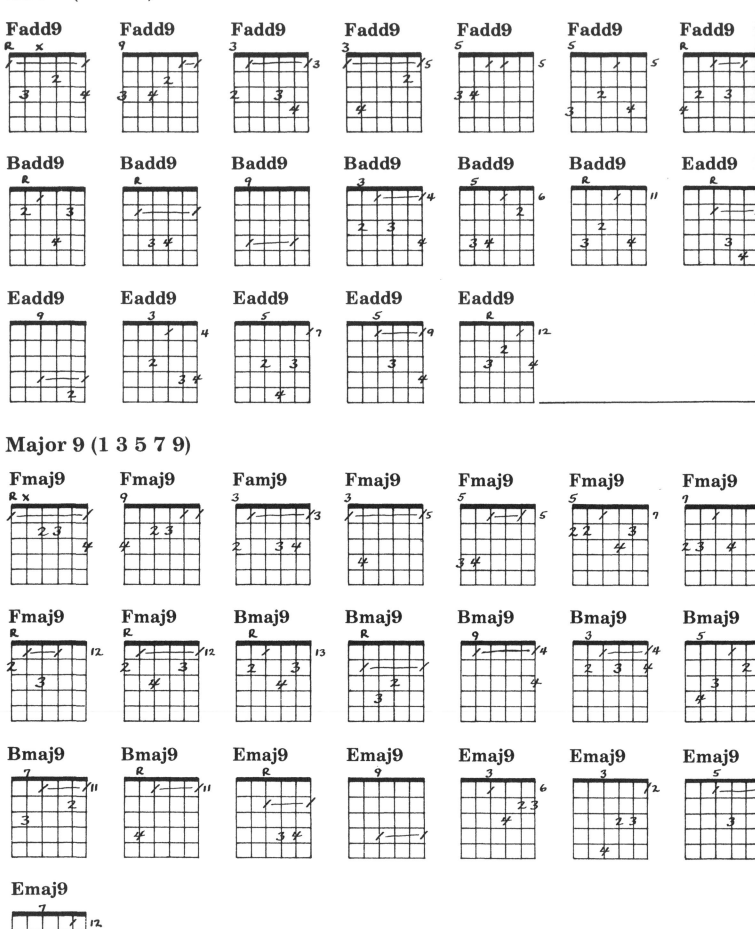

Major 9 (1 3 5 7 9)

Major 9/6 (1 3 5 6 9)

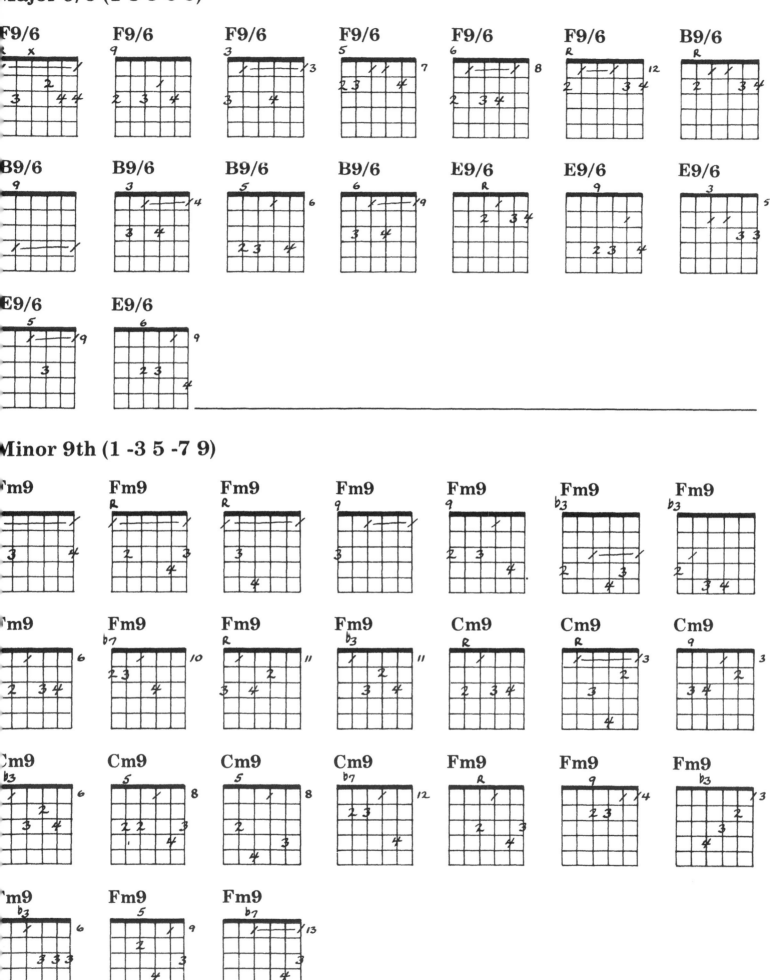

Minor 9th (1 -3 5 -7 9)

31

Minor 9/6 (1 -3 5 6 9)

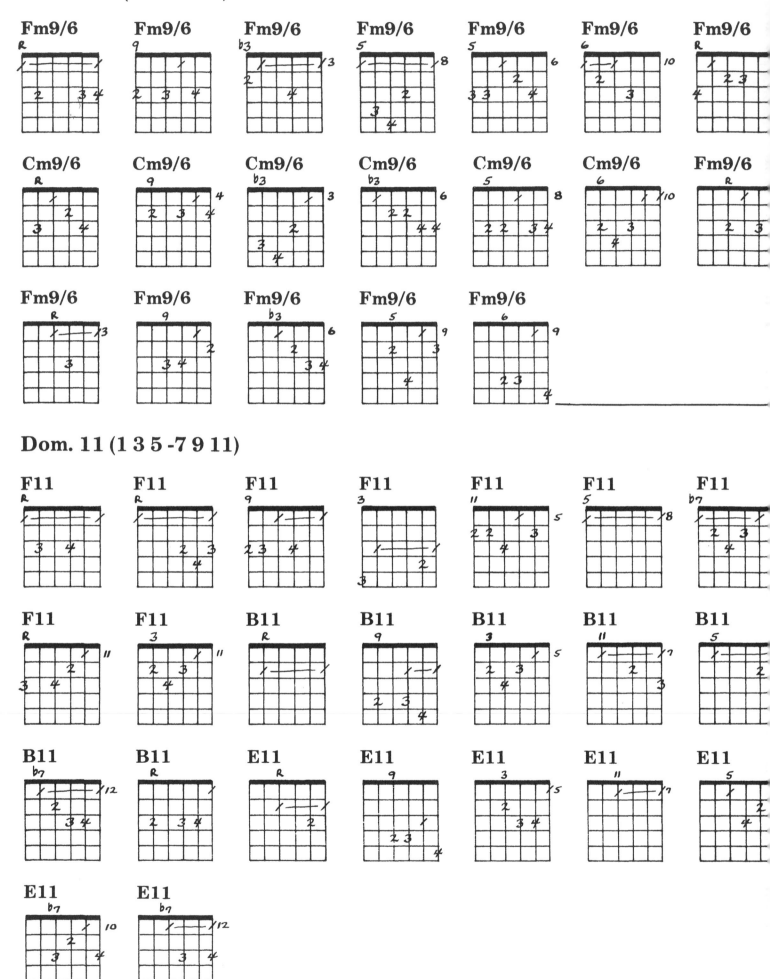

Dom. 11 (1 3 5 -7 9 11)

Aug. 11 (1 3 5 -7 9 #11)

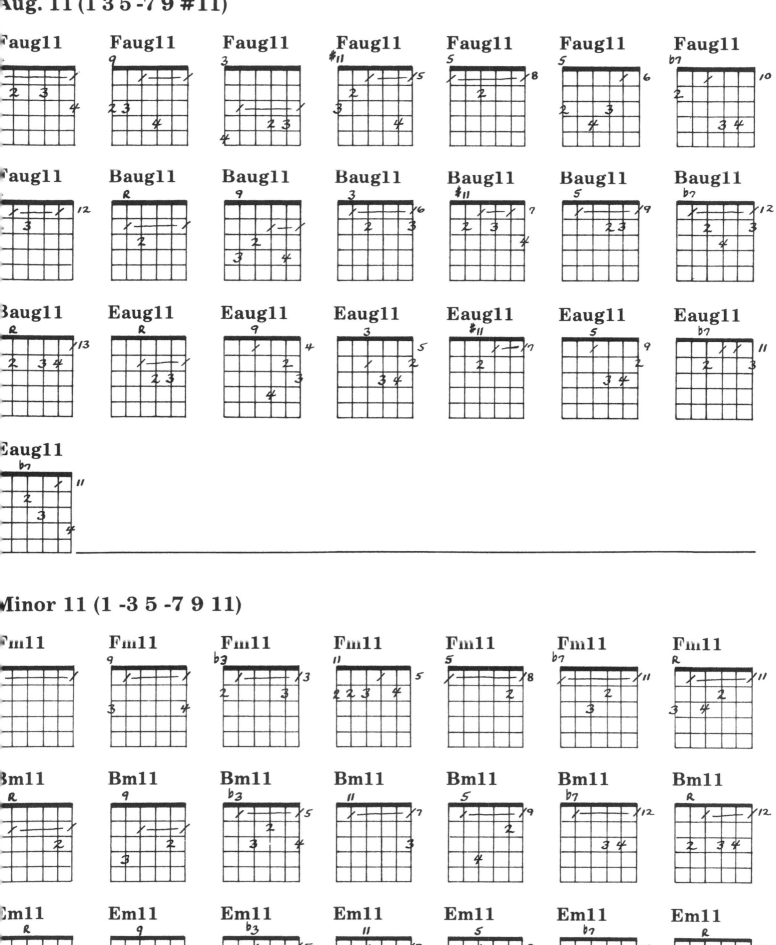

Minor 11 (1 -3 5 -7 9 11)

33

Dom. 13 (1 3 5 -7 9 11 13)

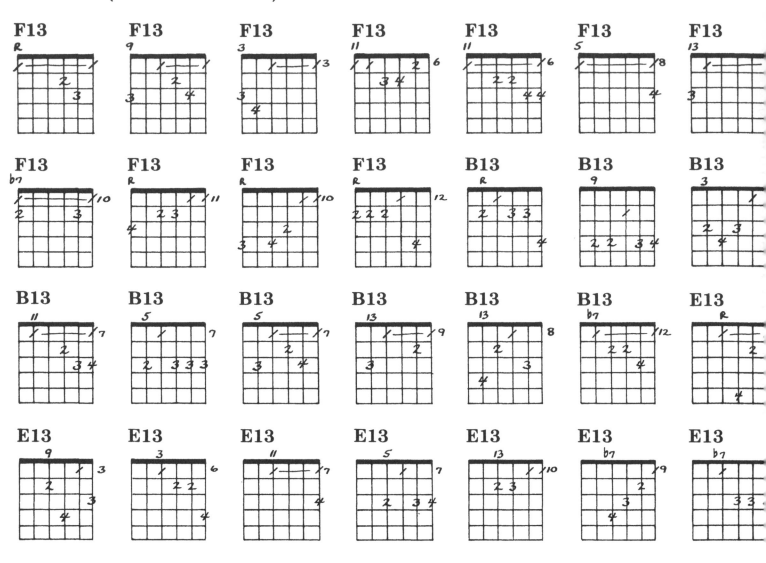

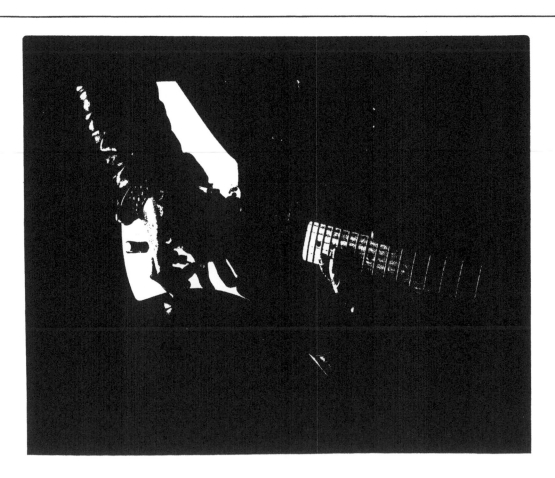

Major 13 (1 3 5 7 9 11 13)

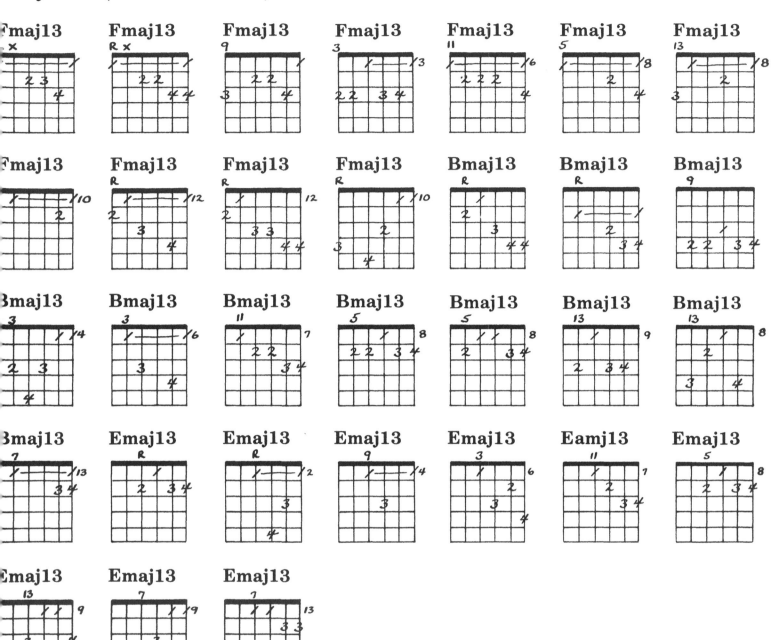

Dom. 13 -9 (1 3 5 -7 -9 11 13)

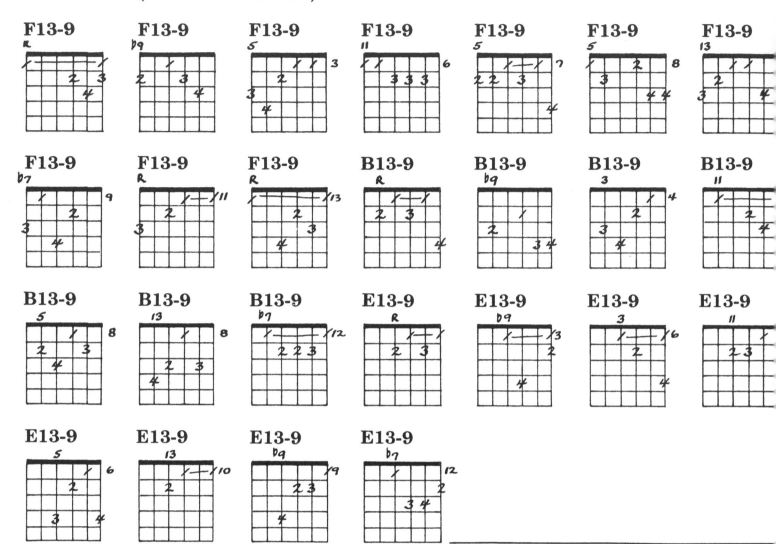

ARPEGGIOS

Arpeggios are broken chords. They utilize only chord tones that are spread out and played melodically. The formulas for the arpeggios are indentical to their corresponding chord formulas.

C MAJOR ARPEGGIO

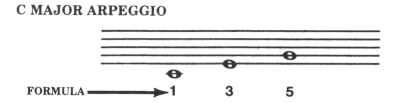

FORMULA ——————▶ 1   3   5

In the following grids on arpeggios, each note should be played separately. Only the root of the arpeggio is identified and like the moveable chords, the root may be placed on any fret making them also moveable to any desired keynote.

Major

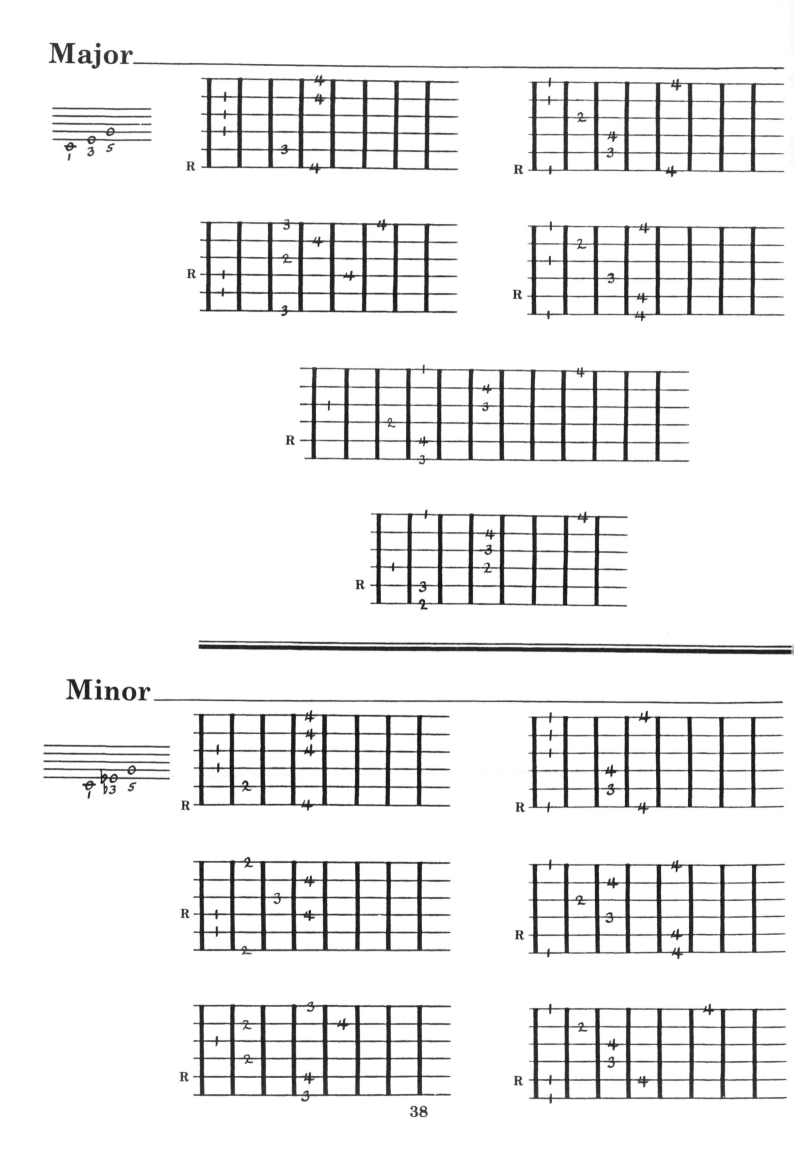

Minor

Augmented

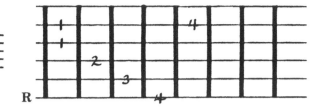 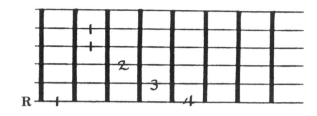

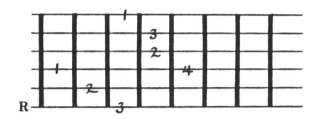 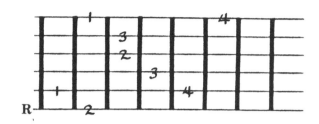

Suspended 4th

 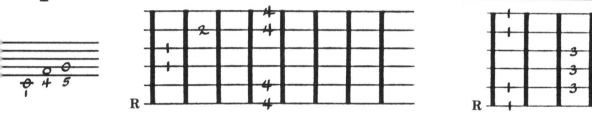 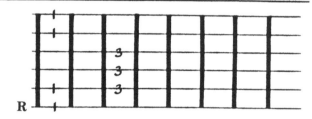

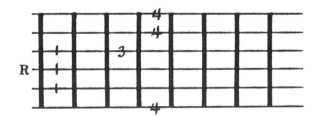 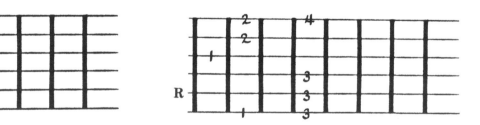

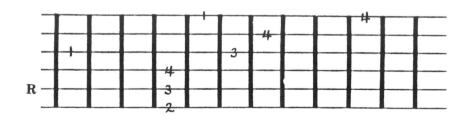

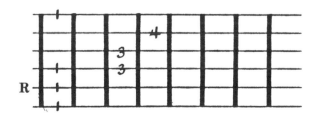

Major6

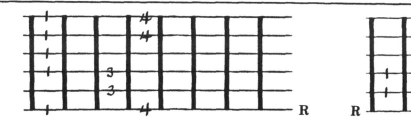

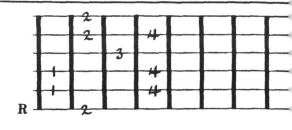

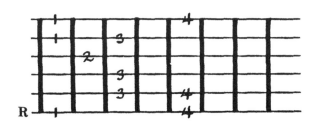

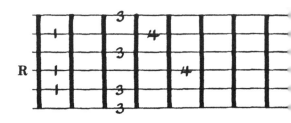

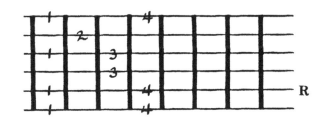

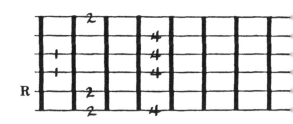

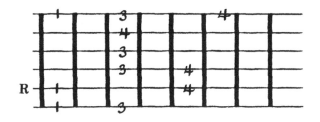

Minor 6

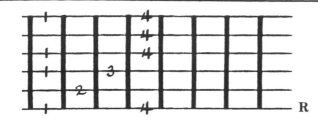
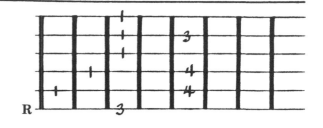

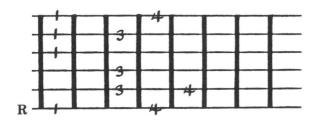
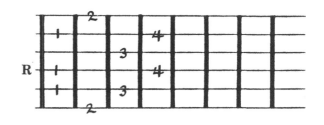

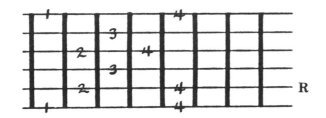
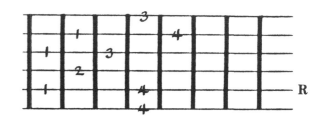

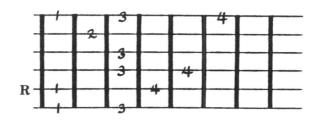

Dom.7

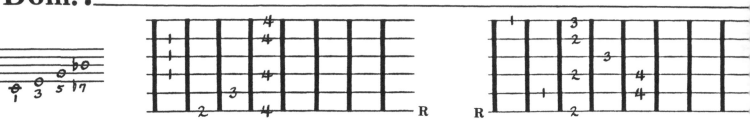

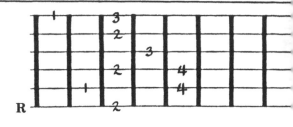

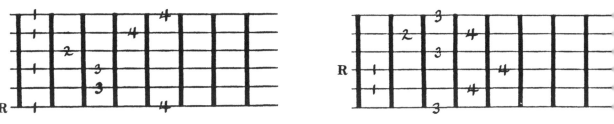

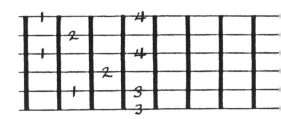

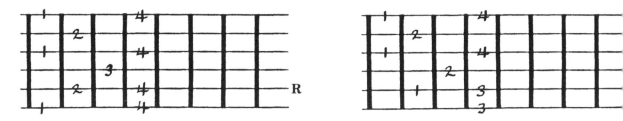

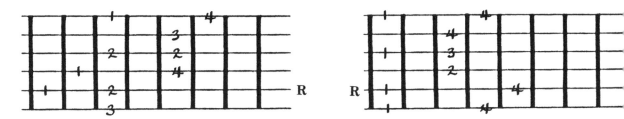

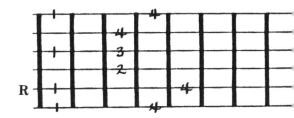

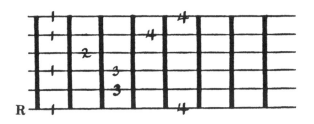

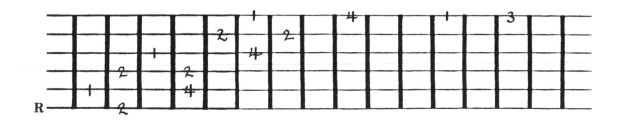

Dom.7th sus.4

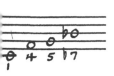

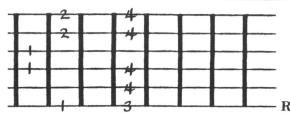
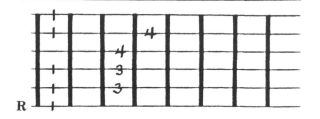

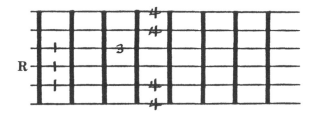
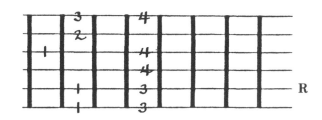

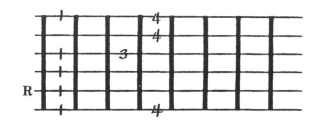

Major7

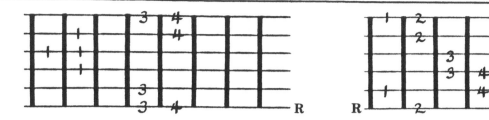

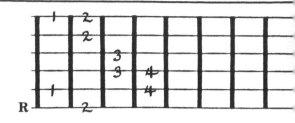

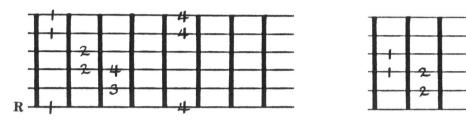

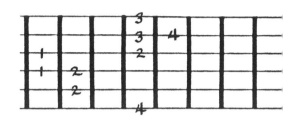

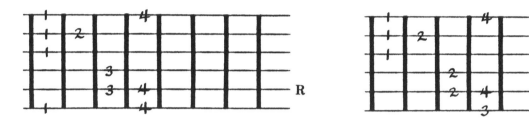

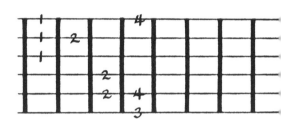

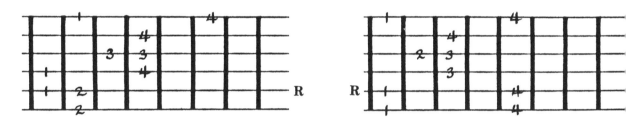

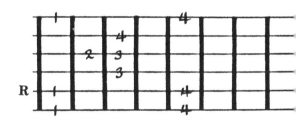

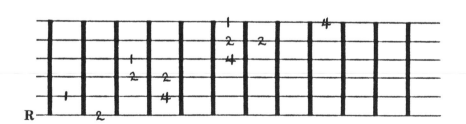

Minor 7

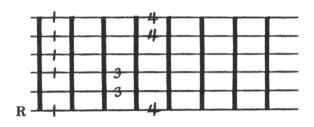
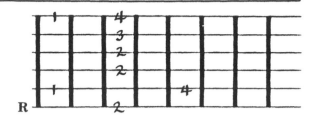

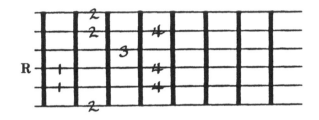
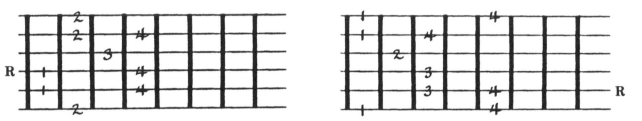

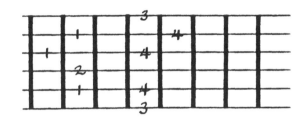
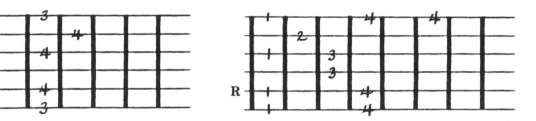

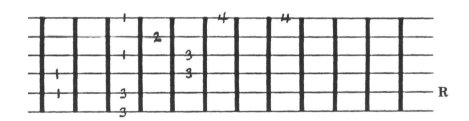

45

Dim.7

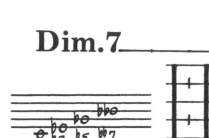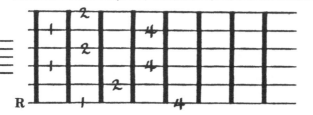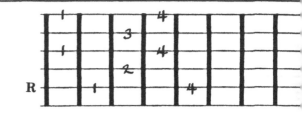

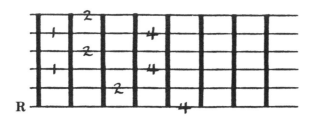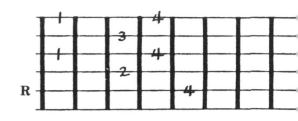

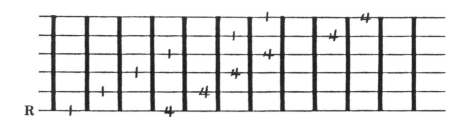

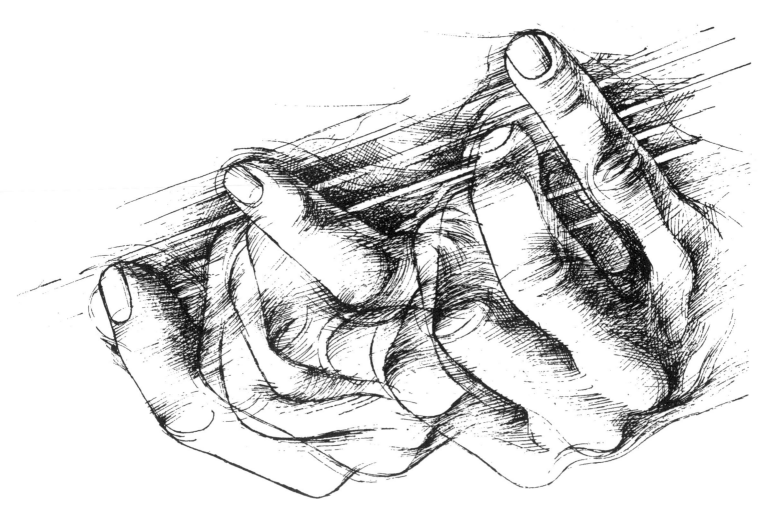

Minor 7-5

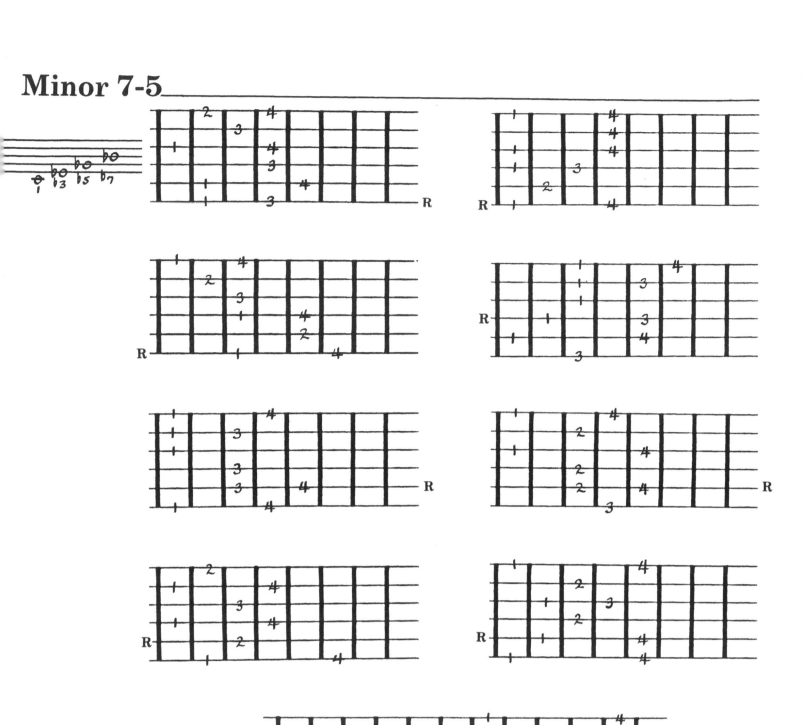

Major 7-5

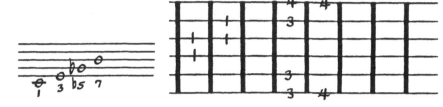

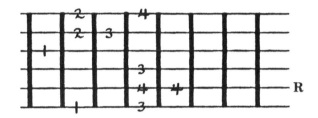

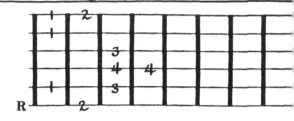

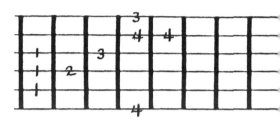

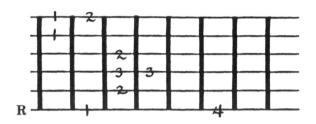

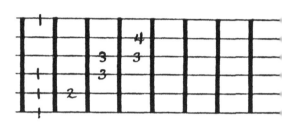

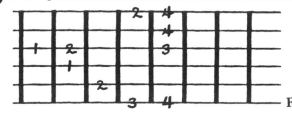
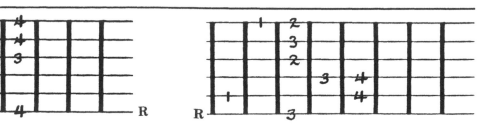

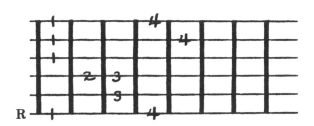
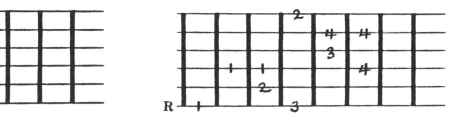

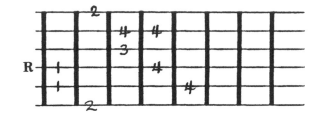
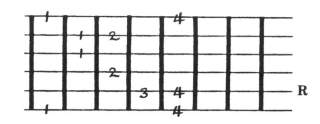

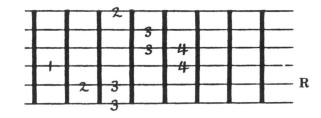
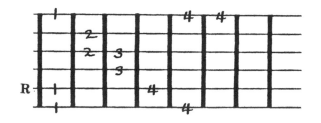

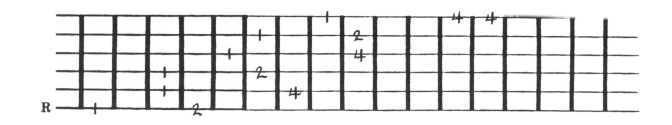

Dom.7#5

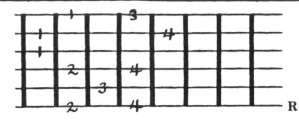 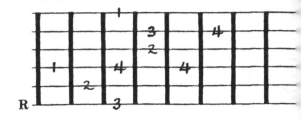

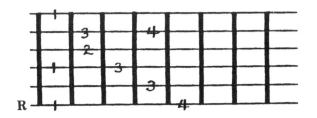 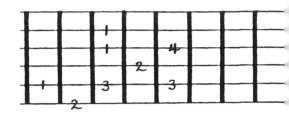

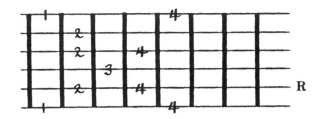 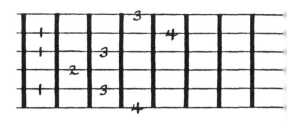

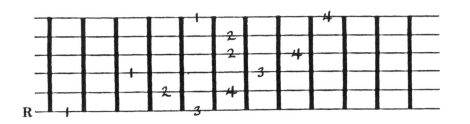

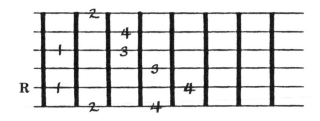

Dom.7 b5

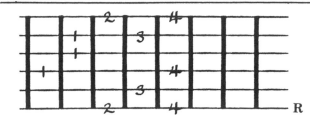
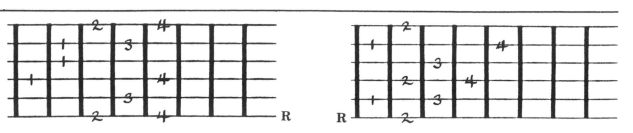

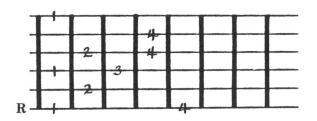
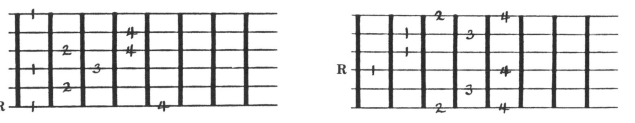

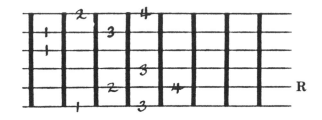
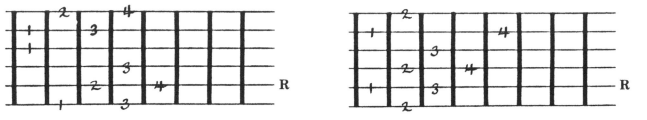

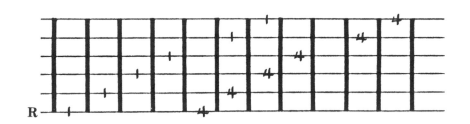

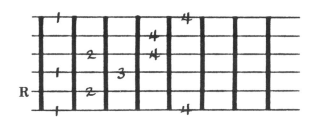

Dom.7b9

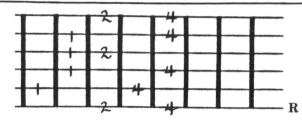

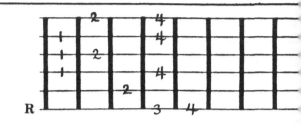

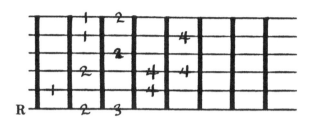

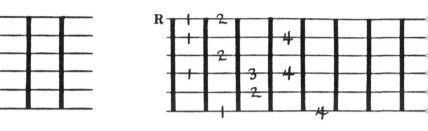

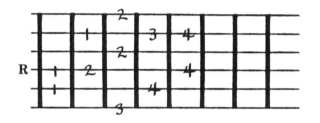

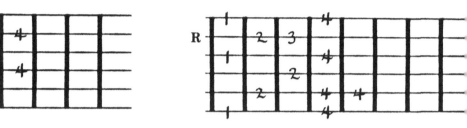

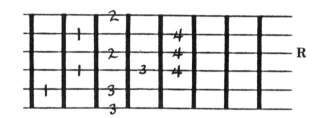

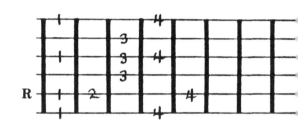

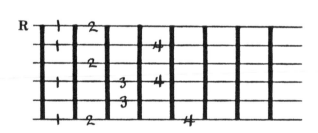

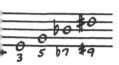
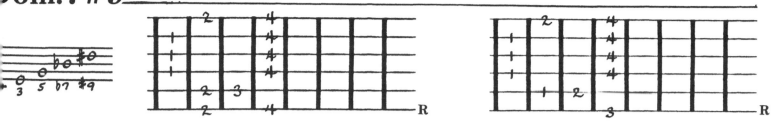
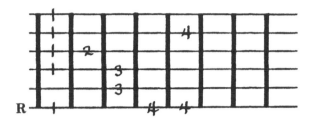
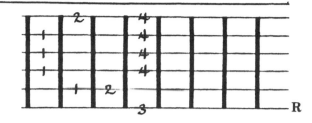
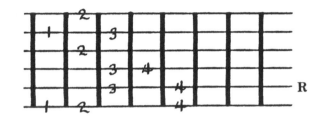
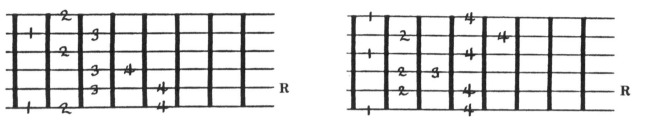
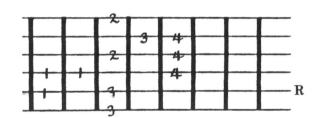
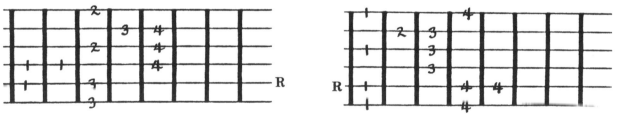
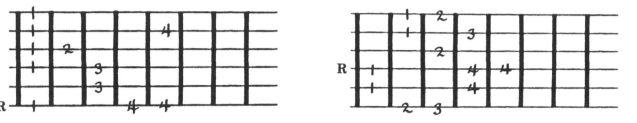

Dom.7#9#5

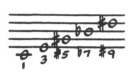

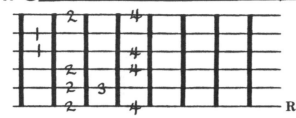
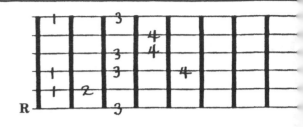

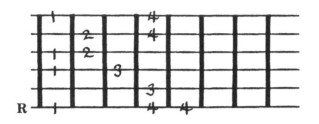
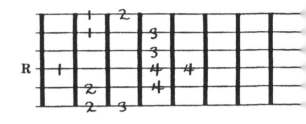

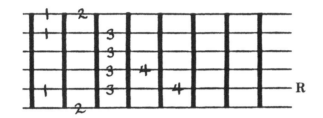
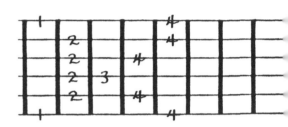

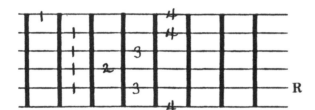
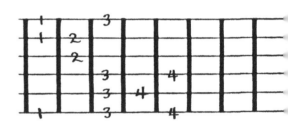

54

Dom.7 #9 b5

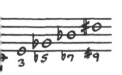

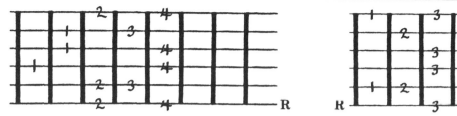

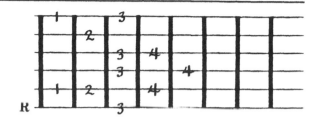

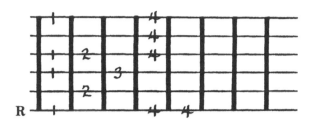

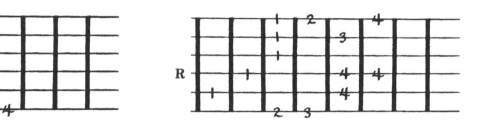

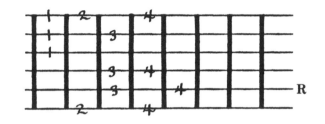

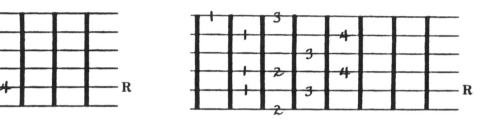

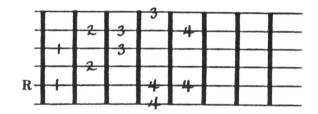

Dom.7 b9#5

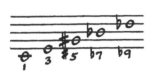

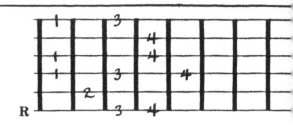

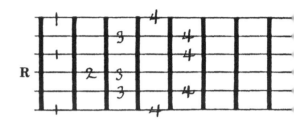

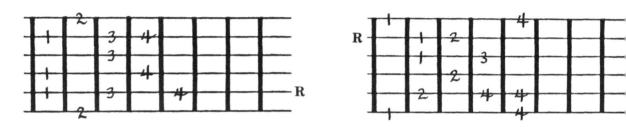

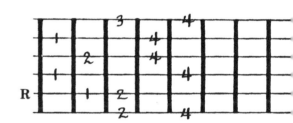

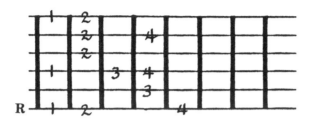

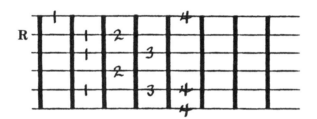

Dom.7 b9 b5

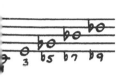

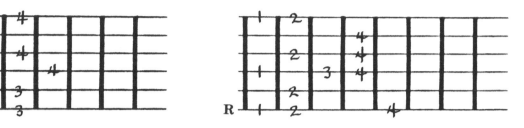

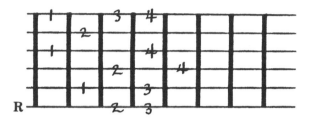

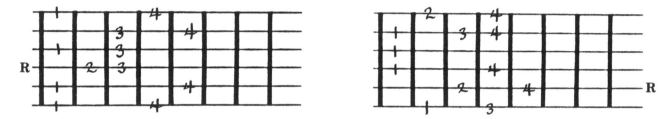

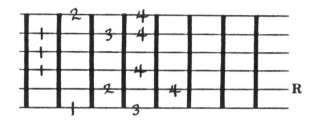

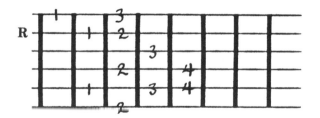

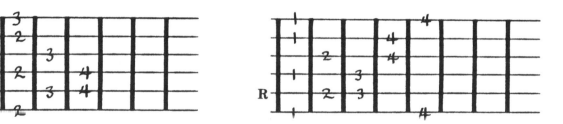

Dom.9

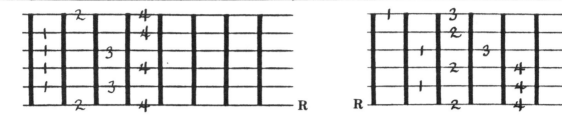

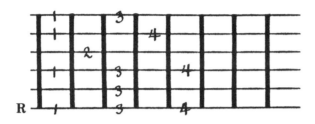 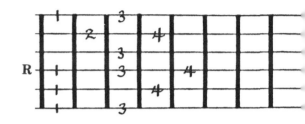

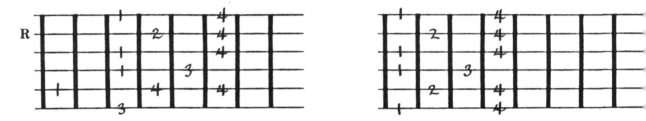 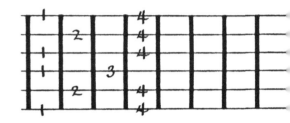

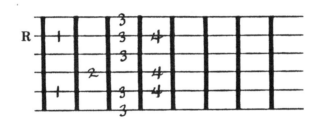 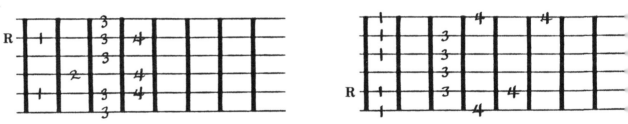

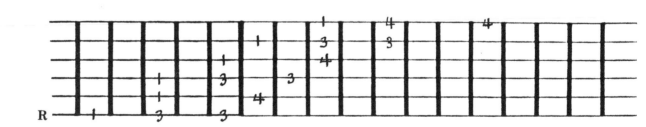

Dom.9 b5

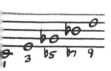

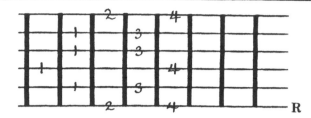

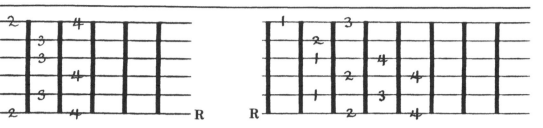

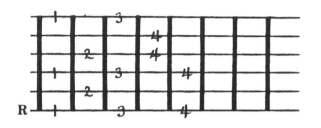

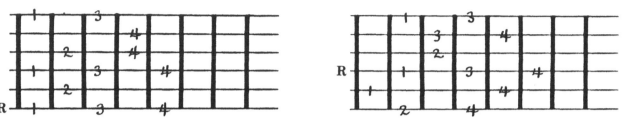

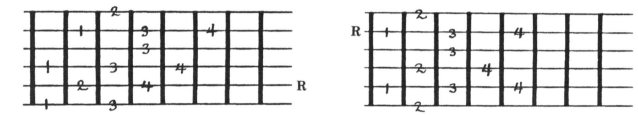

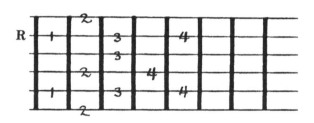

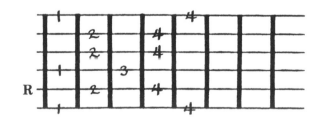

Dom.9#5

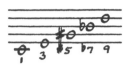

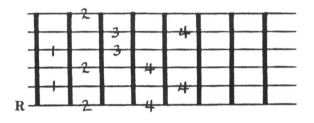

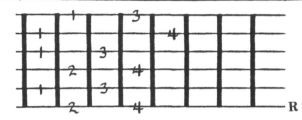
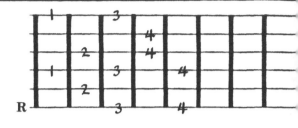

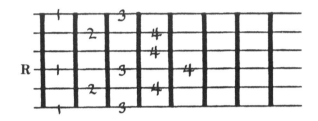
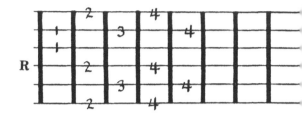

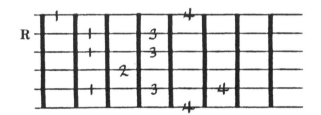
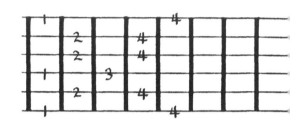

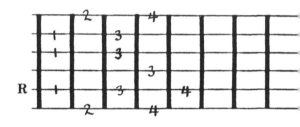

Major add9

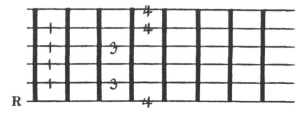
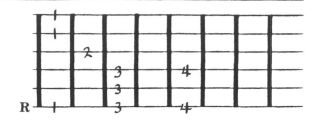

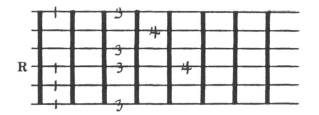
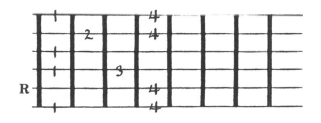

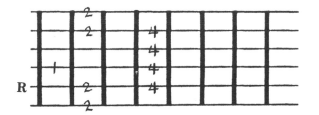
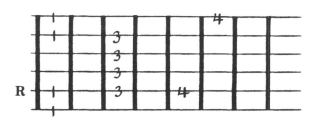

Major 9

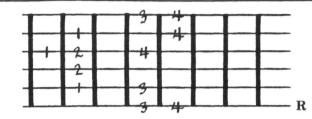
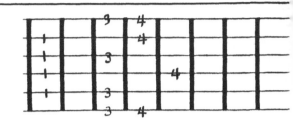

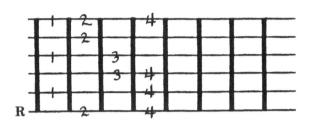
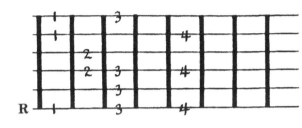

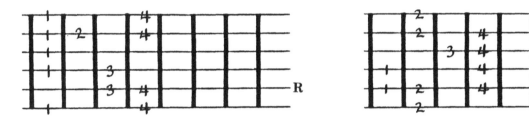
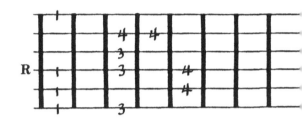
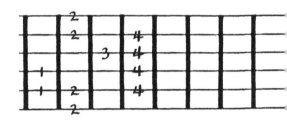

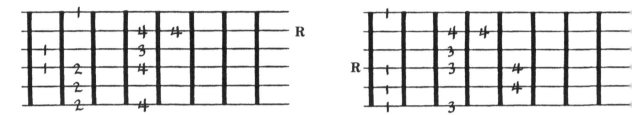

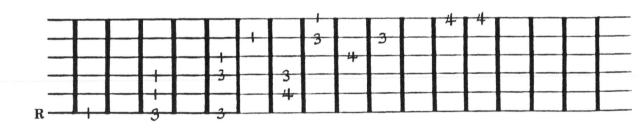

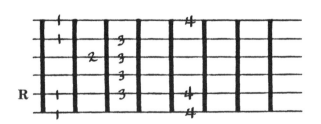

62

Major 9/6

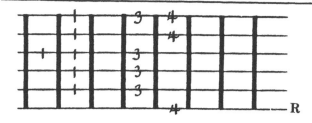 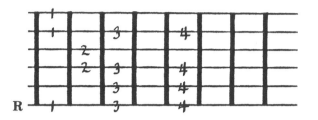 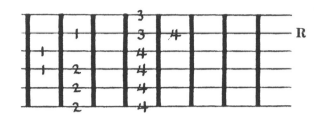

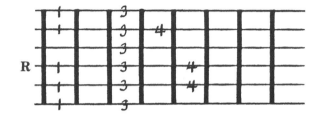 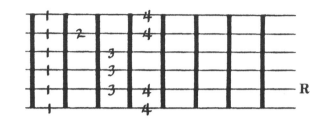

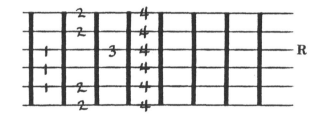 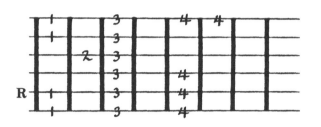

Charlie Christian was 20 years old when he joined the Benny Goodman band in 1939. He revolutionized the electric guitar. The guitar was considered a rhythm instrument until Charlie created an identity for the electric guitar as a solo instrument, playing horn-style, single-note passages in a radical departure from the existing chord-melody approach. He changed forever the way the guitar was played, and then, suffering from tuberculosis, he died in 1943 at the age of 23.

Minor 9

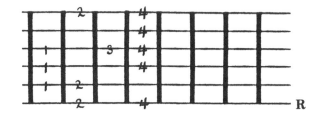

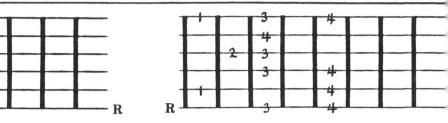

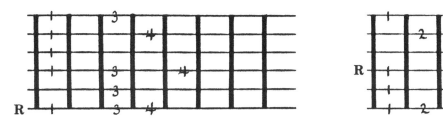

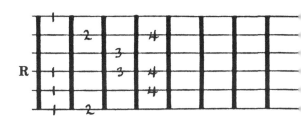

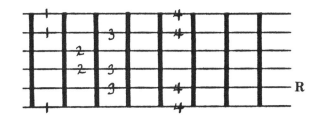

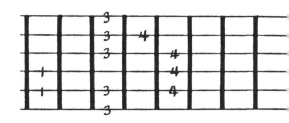

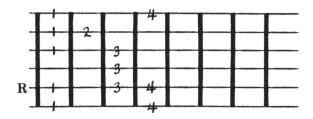

Minor 9/6

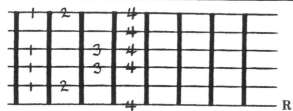
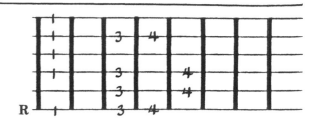

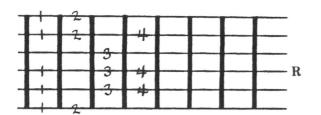
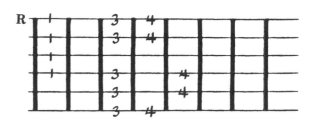

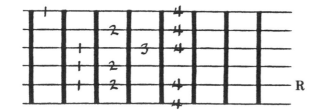
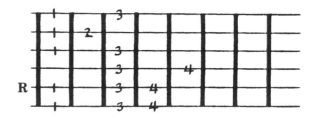

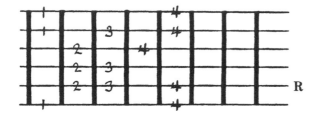
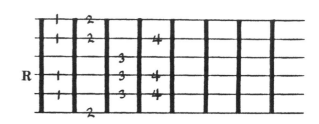

Dom.11

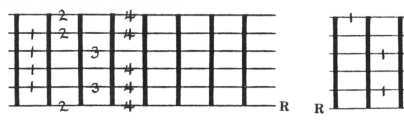

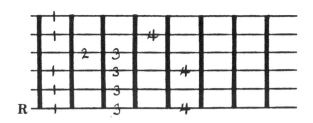

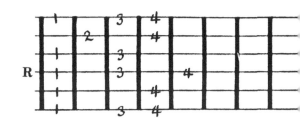

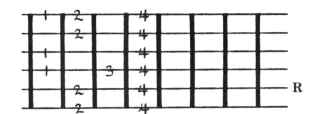

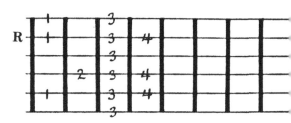

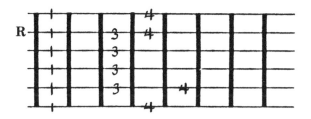

Augmented 11

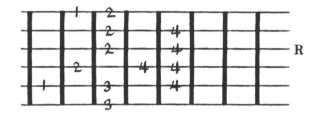
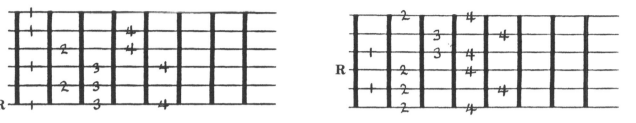
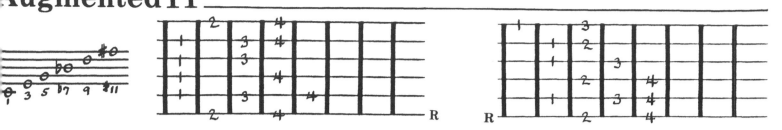
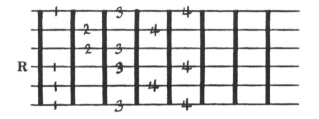
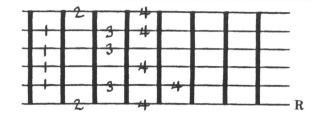
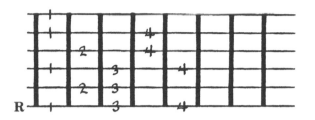
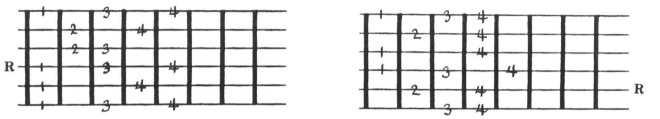
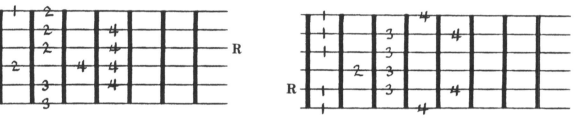
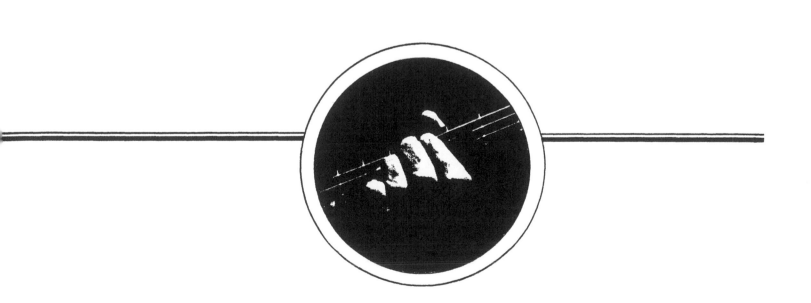

Minor 11

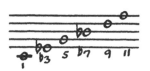

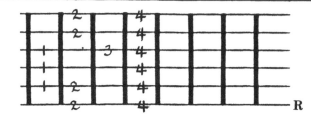

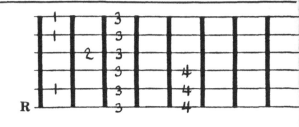

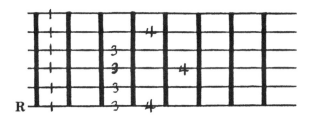

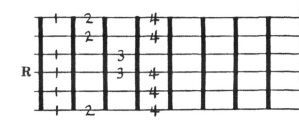

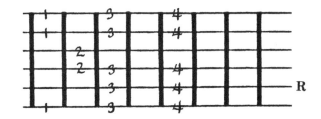

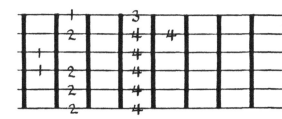

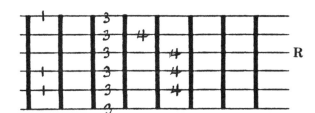

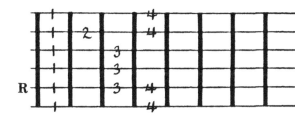

Dom.13

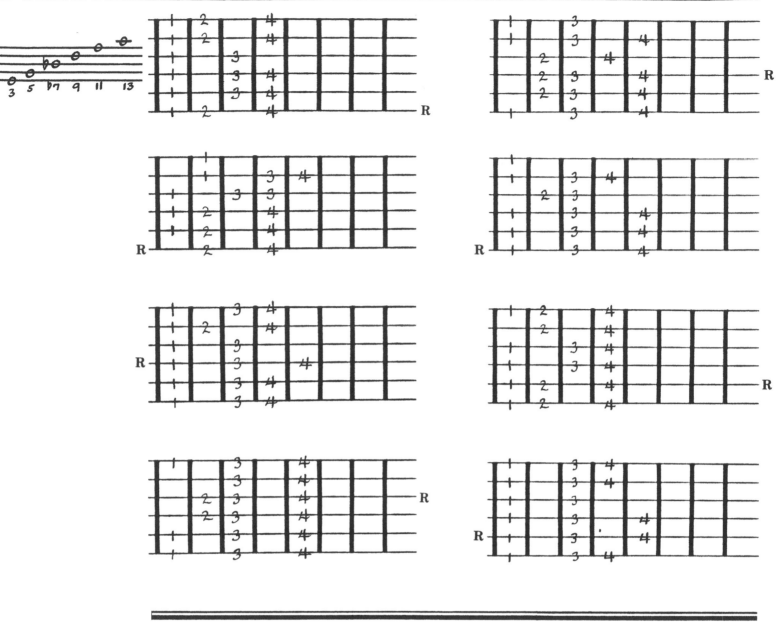

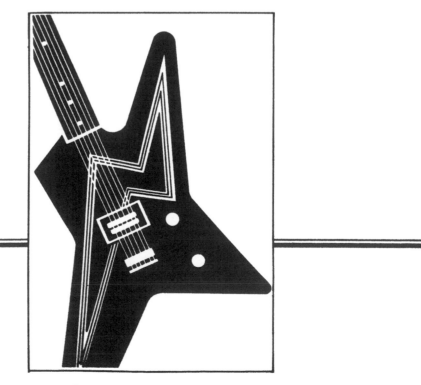

Major 13

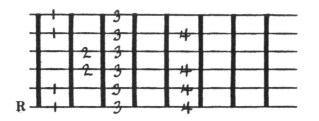

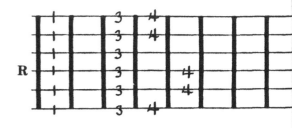

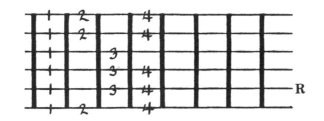

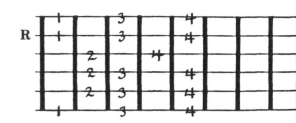

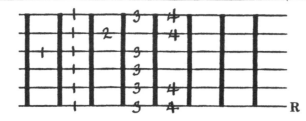

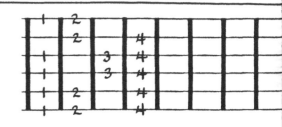

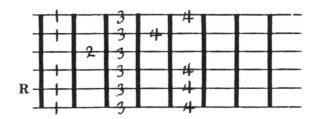

Dom.13 b9

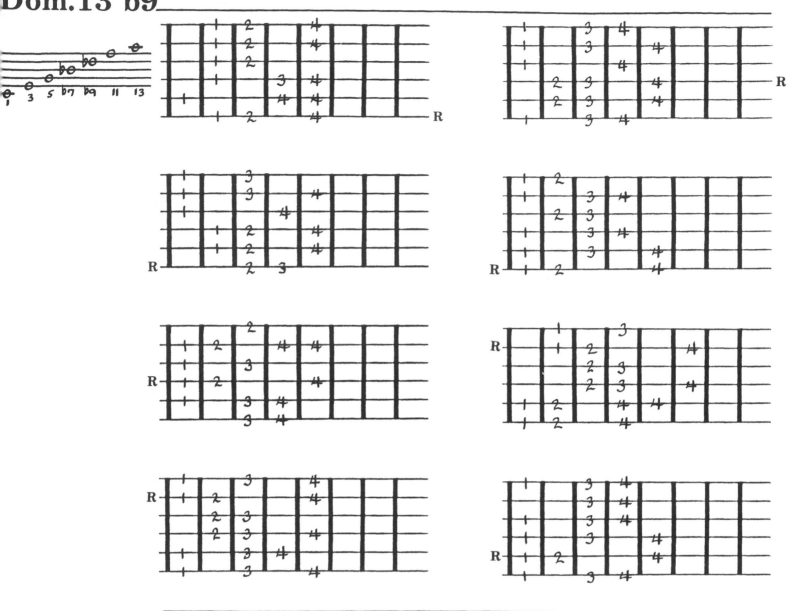

SCALE THEORY

A scale is an ordered set of notes with a particular arrangement of whole (2 frets) and half (1 fret) steps. The major and minor scales are known as tonal scales. The Dorian, Phrygian, Lydian, Mixolydian and Locrian are known as modal scales and were origionally in use particularly in liturgical music up to the seventeenth century. The renewed interest in these modes play a major role in jazz and modern music. It might be noted that the major and natural minor scales are origionally part of the modal scales so their modal names are also indicated.

The Pentatonic scales are probably the oldest of all scales and date back thousands of years in eastern cultures.

The rest of the scales are fabricated scales made to fit specific needs or sounds.

The chart below will outline the scales with their arrangement of whole and half steps. Below each scale the arabic numbering for each tone is indicated including the lowered or raised tones.

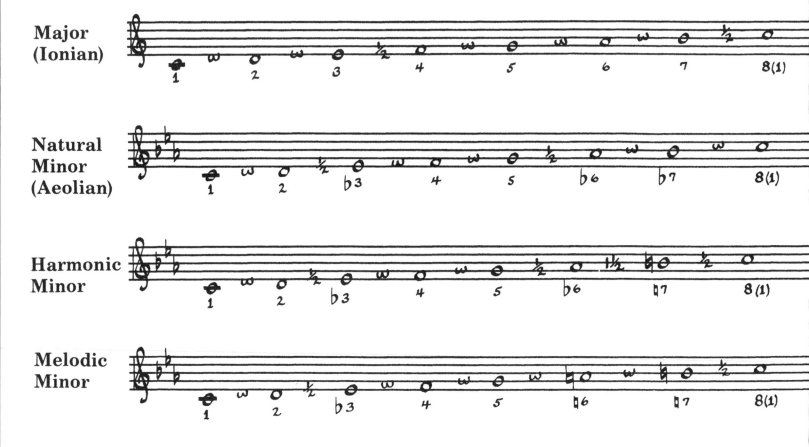

Traditionally, the melodic minor scale will descend with the natural minor scale. The jazz version ascends and descends melodically.

72

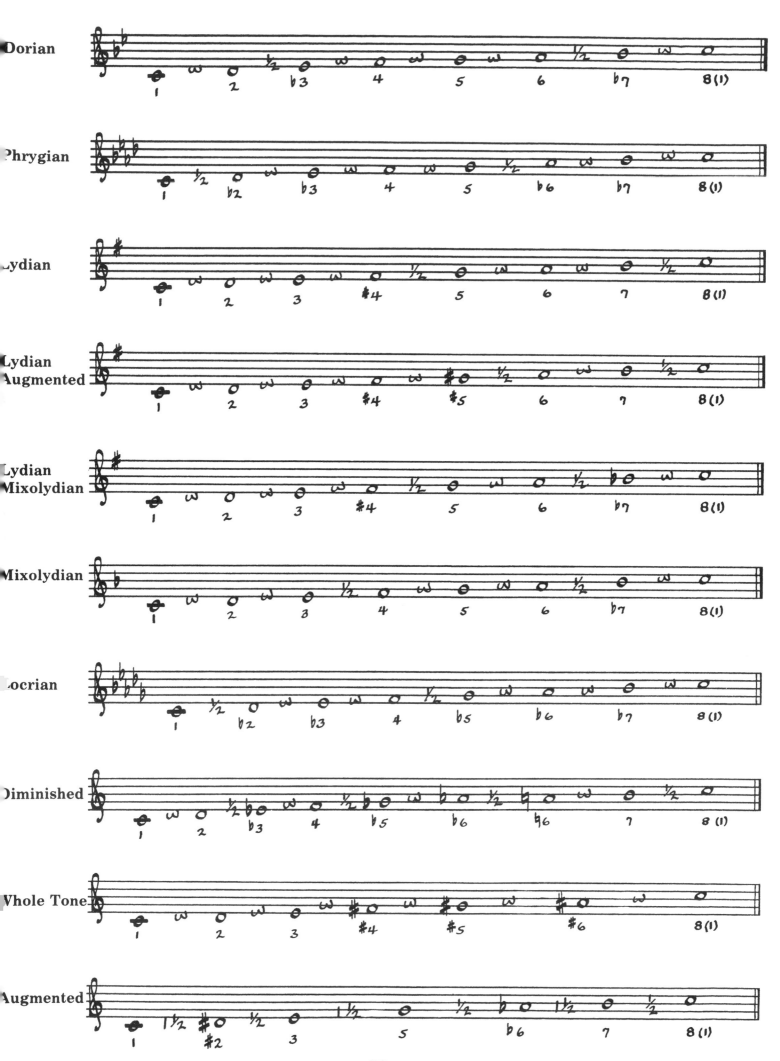

73

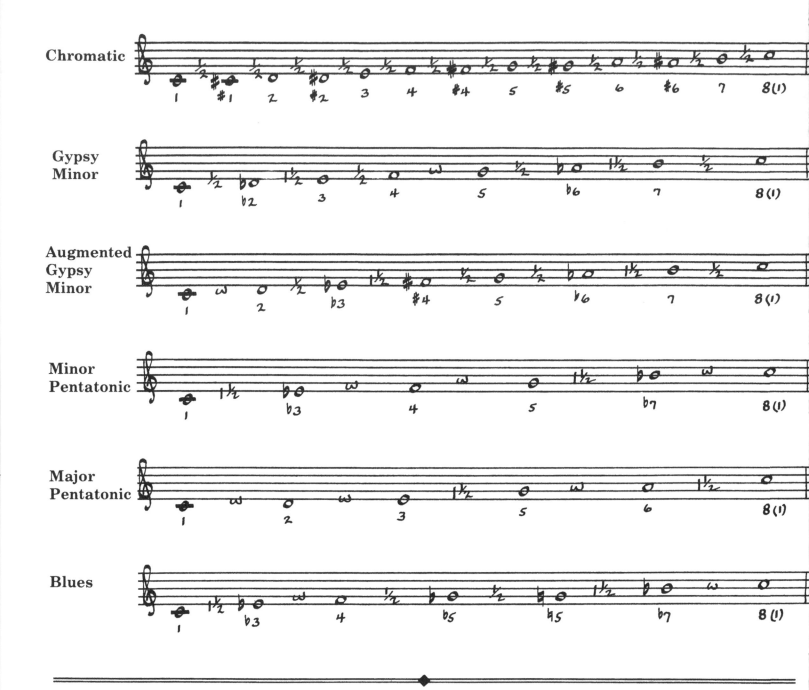

The following scales, like the chords and arpeggios, are completely moveable and each scale can be named by the note with the letter "R" (root).

Major (Ionian)

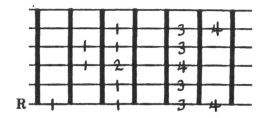

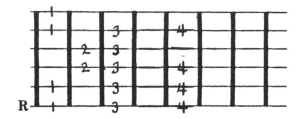

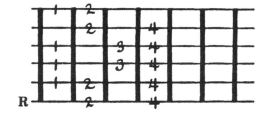

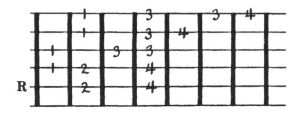

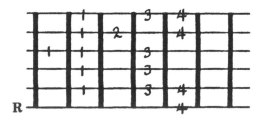

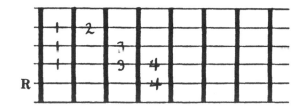

Natural Minor (Aeolian)

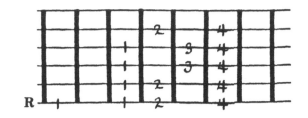

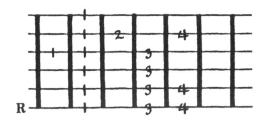

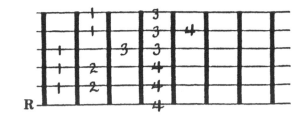

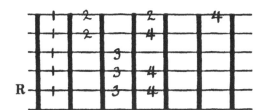

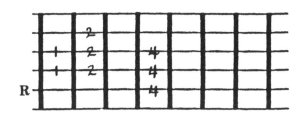

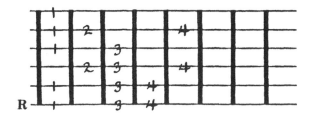

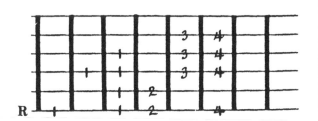

Harmonic Minor

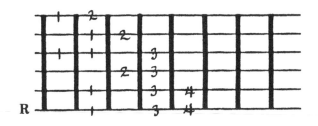

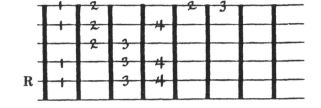

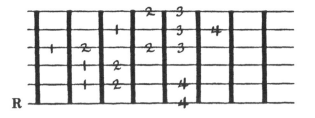

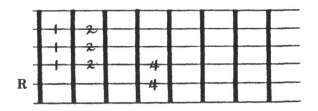

Melodic Minor

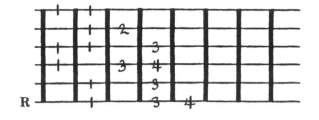

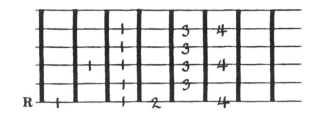

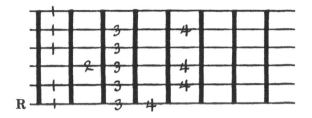

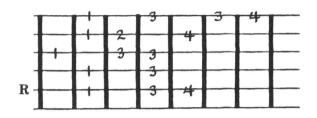

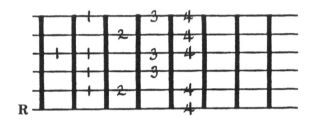

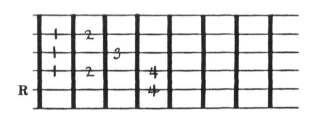

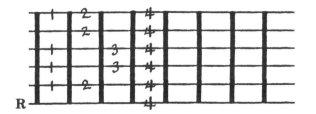

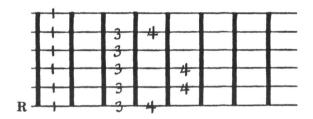

Dorian

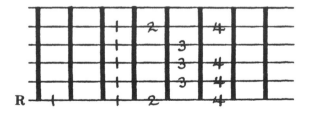

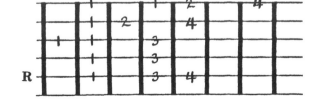

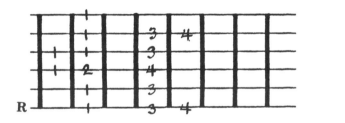

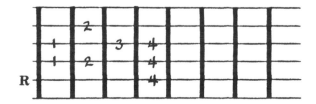

Phrygian

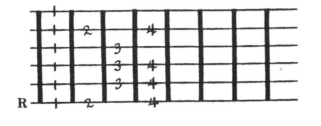
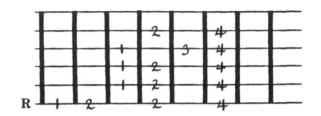

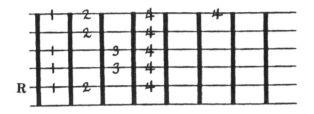
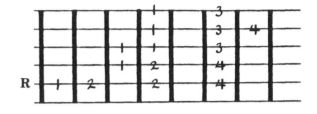

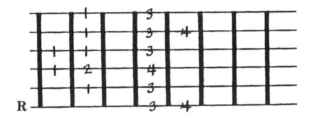
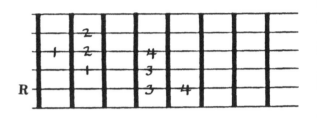

Lydian

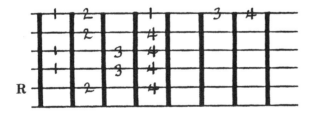
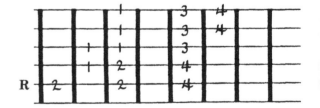

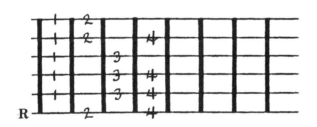
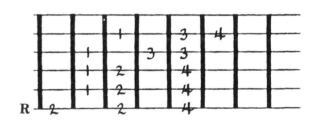

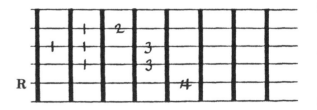
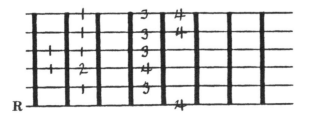

Lydian Augmented

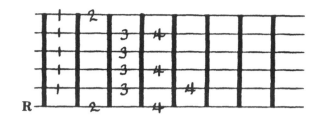

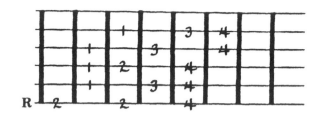

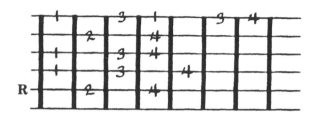

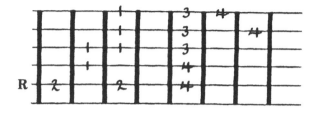

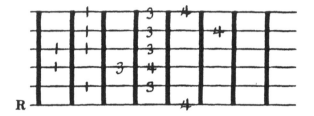

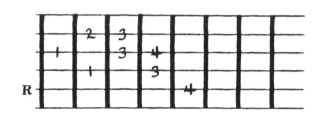

Lydian Mixolydian

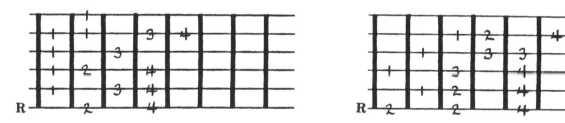

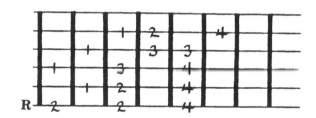

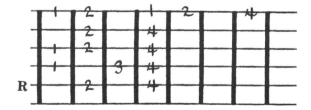

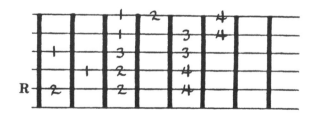

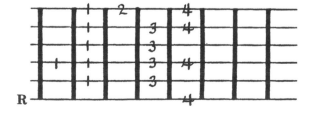

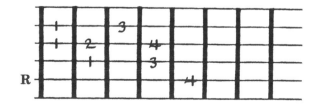

Mixolydian

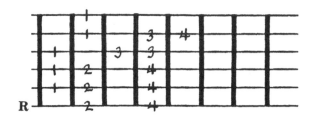 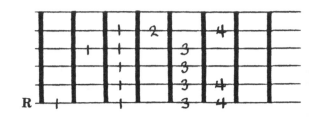

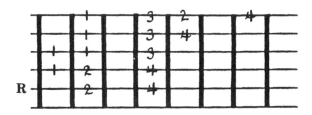 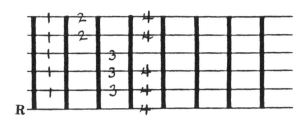

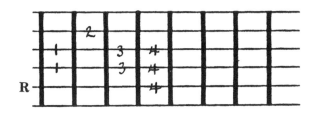

Locrian

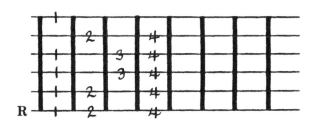 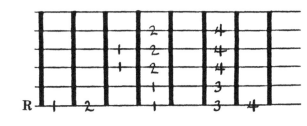

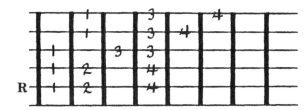 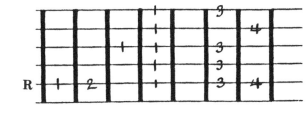

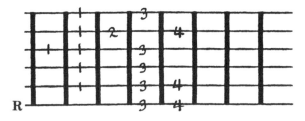 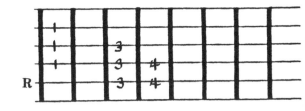

Diminished

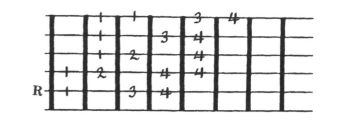

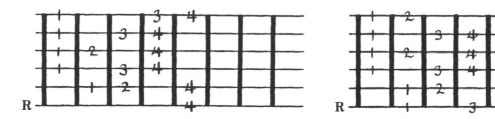 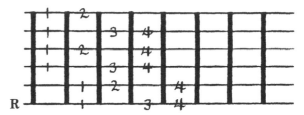

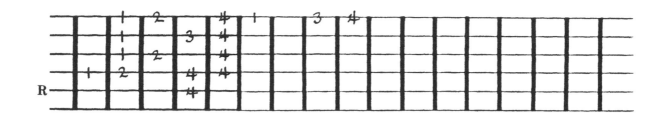

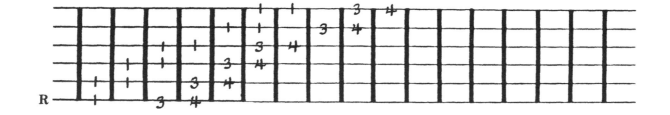

Whole Tone

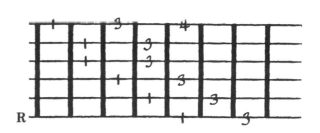

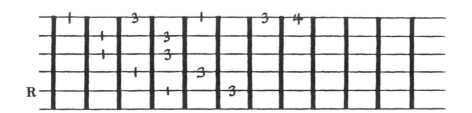

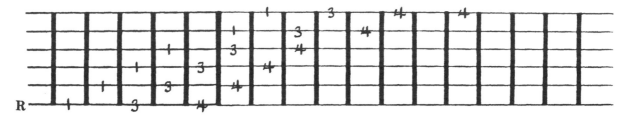

Augmented

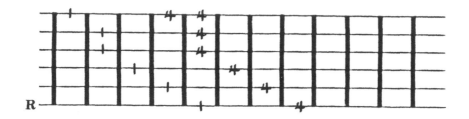

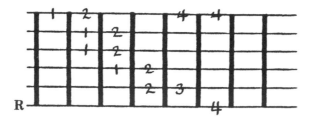

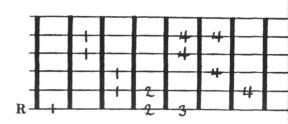

Chromatic

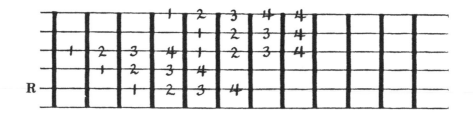

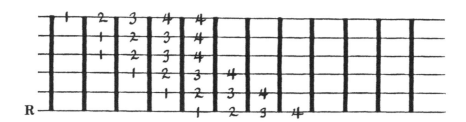

Gypsy Minor

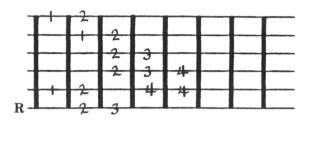
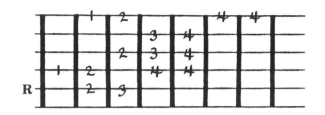

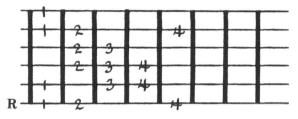
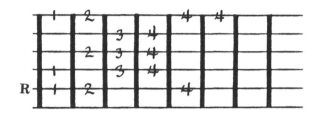

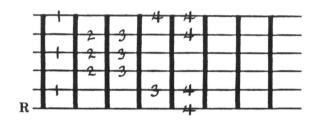
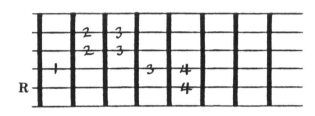

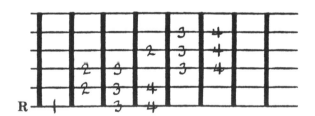
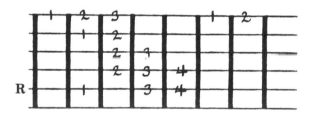

Augmented Gypsy Minor

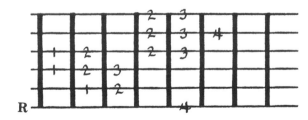

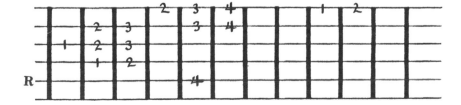

83

Major Pentatonic

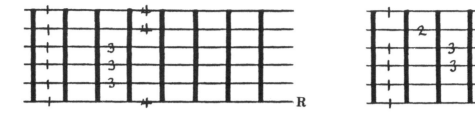

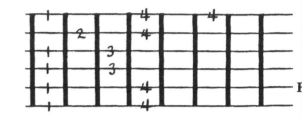

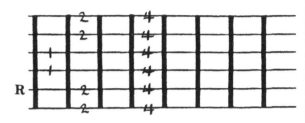

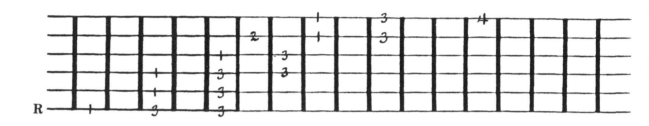

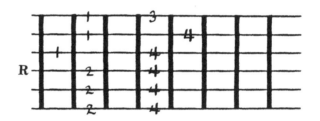

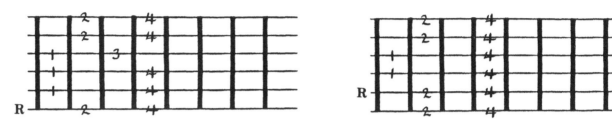

Minor Pentatonic

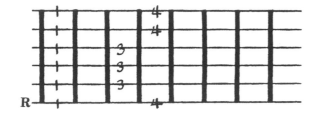

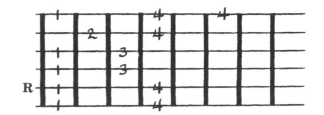

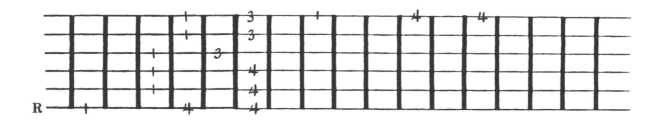

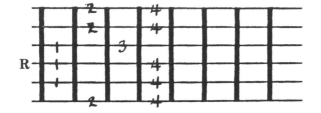

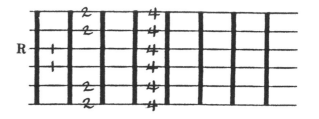

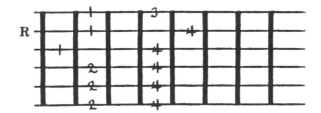

Blues

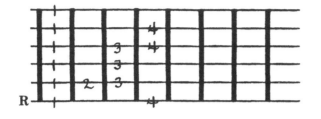 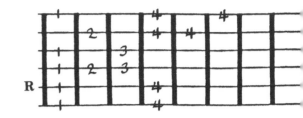

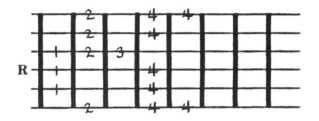 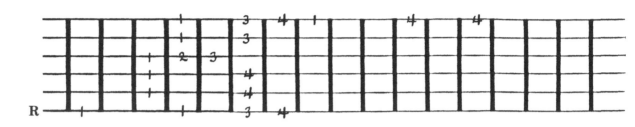

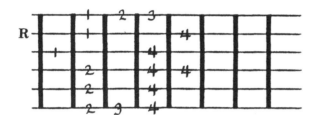 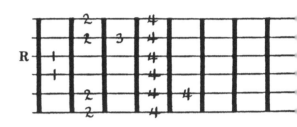

Reverend Gary Davis

Exotic Scales

This next set of scales are not plotted out in this book, but because of their unique sound they are encluded in this section for your own examination.

More Great Guitar Books from Centerstream...